Fine WoodWorking® *on* Spindle Turning

Fine WoodWorking® *on* Spindle Turning

39 articles selected by the editors of *Fine Woodworking* magazine

The Taunton Press

Cover photo by Peter Johnson

Taunton
BOOKS & VIDEOS
for fellow enthusiasts

©1987 by The Taunton Press, Inc.

First printing: January 1987
Second printing: September 1989
Third printing: March 1992
Fourth printing: December 1994
International Standard Book Number: 0-918804-73-6
Library of Congress Catalog Card Number: 86-51290
Printed in the United States of America

A FINE WOODWORKING Book

FINE WOODWORKING® is a trademark of The Taunton Press, Inc.,
registered in the U.S. Patent and Trademark Office.

The Taunton Press, Inc.
63 South Main Street
Box 5506
Newtown, CT 06470-5506

Contents

Introduction

The lathe is the shortest route to a finished wooden part. In fact it is the only small-scale machine that can completely transform a raw piece of tree in one operation: size it, shape it, smooth it and put a finish on it. This is why turned spindles characterize so much Colonial furniture and architecture—in that pre-industrial time, turning was the quickest and easiest way to get the job done. It still is.

In 39 articles reprinted from the first ten years of *Fine Woodworking* magazine, authors who are also craftsmen demonstrate the vast variety of useful things that can be turned between centers. (A companion volume, *Faceplate Turning*, deals exclusively with turned wooden bowls.) They show you exactly how to use the turner's gouge, and how to master one of the most difficult of all tools, the skew chisel. Here too are compendiums of crafty shop tips, plans for useful tools and gauges to make, and revealing looks at such turned specialties as porch pillars, baseball bats and lacemaking bobbins. And finally, there are a couple of strategies for achieving the look of turned wood without a lathe.

John Kelsey, editor

Spindle Turning

How to sharpen and use roughing-down and coving gouges

by Peter Child

For turning between centers, standard roughing-down gouges and coving gouges are best. These spindle gouges have only two shapes of blade. The roughing-down tool has a deep, U-shaped flute ground straight across with no pointed nose, and the coving gouge has a shallower flute with a pointed "lady's fingernail" nose.

Roughing-down gouges have an even thickness of metal all around the cutting edge and a very short single bevel of 45°. Unlike bowl gouges, they have no keel. Three sizes are commonly available: ¾ in., 1 in. and 1¼ in. The first and last sizes should both be the choice of the turner if possible; the 1-in. size is the economy combination tool.

Coving (spindle) gouges have a longer bevel than roughing-down gouges. Four sizes will handle all the turner's requirements: ¼ in., ⅜ in., ½ in. and ¾ in. Any work requiring larger coves, hollows or long curves can be done better with roughing-down gouges, so gouges larger than ¾ in. aren't necessary. Both roughing-down and coving gouges should have long, heavy-duty handles to facilitate control—mine are at least 10 in. long.

Gouges are cutting tools. They fashion a cove or hollow by cutting down from each side alternately until the desired shape is reached. A gouge is rarely the exact size of a desired cut. A customer of mine complained that a ¾-in. gouge supplied was in fact ¹³⁄₁₆ in. and consequently of no use to him. He was obviously misusing the gouge as a forming tool, pushing it straight into the revolving wood and scraping out a hollow which he required to be exactly ¾ in. across. Using a

gouge as a scraper is wrong. An important woodturning principle is that cutting tools always work from large diameter to small: Revolving wood cannot be properly cut "uphill." This means that the tool must have room to work, especially at the bottom of the cove, so it is impossible to cut a ¾-in. cove with a ¾-in. gouge. It would be better to use a ½-in. gouge.

Most woodworking tools are properly shaped by the factory grinder and finisher, and sharpening is all that is needed before using them. Woodturning tools are an exception and have remained so, despite the efforts of professional turners to educate manufacturers. So be very critical regarding the shape and bevel length of brand-new gouge blades. You may find that a roughing-down gouge is not ground straight across, a condition which must be remedied on the grindstone. The bevel length will almost certainly be too long, not the correct angle of 45°. Sometimes a lot of metal (and money) has to be ground away before the correct angle is reached. As a temporary measure, a very short 45° angle can be ground on the longer bevel. This is against another basic woodturning principle, which is that no tool has more than one bevel on the cutting edge. Successive grindings, however, will eventually get down to one bevel of 45°. Do not try this dodge on new coving gouges.

The grindstone is an important tool in the turner's shop and should be used not only as a "grind" stone but as a "sharpening" stone. The grit grade must not be so coarse that a sharp edge cannot be ground, or so fine that an edge can easily be burned at the tip. A good medium grit is a Carborundum (silicon carbide) dry wheel A54-N5-V30W or an equivalent grade. The diameter should not exceed 7 in. and the width should be at least 1 in. The stone should revolve towards the user at the fastest speed possible, although not

Master turner Peter Child, author of The Craftsman Woodturner *(rev. ed., Sterling Publishing) and once a production woodturner, teaches in Halstead, England.*

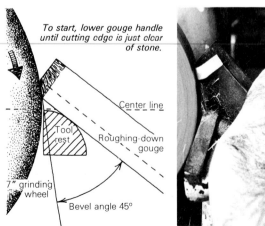  

To start, lower gouge handle until cutting edge is just clear of stone.

Center line

Tool rest

Roughing-down gouge

7" grinding wheel

Bevel angle 45°

To sharpen a roughing-down gouge, hold the blade on the rest and lower the handle until the cutting edge is just clear of the stone. Roll the bevel slowly from side to side, keeping the point of contact at right angles to the stone. As the bevel comes up (photo sequence), *the bright mark shows the operator for the first time where he is removing metal. Lift or lower the handle until the center of the bevel is reached, then continue to roll the blade with no variation in height until the bevel starts to hollow out and fit the stone.*

From *Fine Woodworking* magazine (September 1978) 12:60-64

faster than the safety rpm marked on its side. Safety glasses are a must, but provided the stone is maintained and used as described, I don't find other guards essential.

The stone must be kept to its original shape and completely free from dirt, swarf and glazing. As an example, after, say, three new tools have been shaped and sharpened, the stone will need cleaning. This is achieved with either a diamond or star-wheel dressing tool. The latter is much cheaper and just as effective.

Hollow grinding is when the whole of the bevel of the tool, from heel to sharp edge, is in full contact with the stone's circular surface, and thus takes on the negative contour of the stone. Grinding has to stop at the exact moment the cutting edge of the tool comes in contact with the stone. This sounds simple but when I watch my pupils trying to do it I realize how frustrating doing this properly is to learn.

Beginners at grinding usually make several common mistakes. First, they hold the tool far too firmly and stiffly when approaching the stone. The more relaxed hold is with one hand over the tool, holding it down on the rest, with just the fingers of the other hand around the handle. There should be just enough firmness to hold the tool in place. An efficient stone of the right grit will do its work all by itself and need not be pushed. Pressure leads quickly to burning, whereas with no pressure the tool can be rested on the running stone for considerable time before it even gets hot.

Inclining the head to one side to see if the tool is being presented at the proper angle is another common fault. There is little control when watching from the side. The head and eyes should always be directly behind the blade and handle.

Another fault—lifting the blade off two or three times to inspect it—results in the bevel surface looking like a badly plowed field. It is almost impossible to replace the blade at the exact grindstone height from which it is taken.

Roughing-down gouges

With a roughing-down gouge we are grinding a straight-across edge, and it is important to roll the blade so that at all times it is at right angles to the stone. With a right-handed operator, his right hand on the handle keeps the tool at this angle, and his eyes on the edge tell his hand what handle adjustments to make. The diagram and photos show how to proceed. A stream of sparks traveling on top of the flute indicates that the edge has been reached, and I advise beginners to stop right before or just at this point. What happens is that the edge is broken into thousands of little cutting burrs or sawteeth, like a tiny breadknife or steak knife. Such an edge works well in woodturning and when blunt is quickly and easily resharpened. Over-grinding the edge produces only comparatively few thick burrs, easily broken and blunted by the revolving wood. To avoid over-grinding, stop as soon as the sparks travel on top of the edge. Then the operator should point the gouge straight at his face and look directly at the edge. The places that reflect light have not yet been reached by the sparks. After two or three more careful passes on the stone, these areas of light should have disappeared and the edge will be sharp. Another test is to feel around the inside of the flute with a fingertip. There should be a minute roughness all around. I now go directly to the lathe, without any attention from the oilstone, where the tool cuts efficiently for a short time before it needs to be resharpened. When this is required, the heel of the bevel is put into contact with the stone

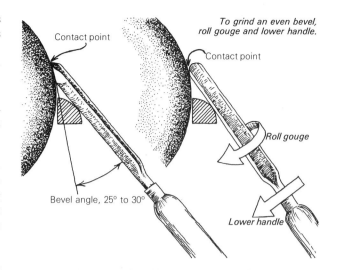

To grind an even bevel, roll gouge and lower handle.

Contact point

Contact point

Roll gouge

Bevel angle, 25° to 30°

Lower handle

Start sharpening a coving gouge at the center, then roll the blade over to the left while lowering the handle, as in the drawing. The blade rides up so that its left edge contacts the stone at the same height the center did. Then roll to the right the same way (photos top and above left). To hone by hand (photo, right), brace the gouge against the lathe and move the stone around the bevel. Keep the stone in firm contact with the point and heel.

and the handle is gradually lifted until the sparks appear at the edge—it takes just a few seconds.

The beginner, who should stop grinding just before the hollowing-out bevel meets the cutting edge, should hand-hone to a finish with a flat medium to fine oilstone, keeping it firmly in contact with the heel of the bevel and the edge of the tool, in a dead straight plane without any rocking motion. The partly hollow-ground bevel will save time in sharpening, because there is less metal to remove than if the bevel were totally flat. The tool can be used for a considerable period, hand-honing at frequent intervals until the hollow in the bevel almost disappears. Then it must be formed again. A completely hollow-ground tool is perfect, a dead straight bevel is good, but the slightest trend towards a "belly" or roundness of the bevel means the tool is useless.

Coving gouges

I have a "black-iron" coving gouge, entirely handmade before I was born, which is a beautiful tool to use. The underside is slightly more than a half of a circle in shape and a finger moves around it smoothly without hindrance. Imagine a pencil cut lengthwise down just above the diameter; the bigger portion would be the same shape as my gouge. A gouge works with a rolling or scooping action, depending on the task, so it should be obvious that the fully rounded pencil shape is ideal for both purposes, the underside offering no resistance to the edge of the tool rest.

Nowadays, for cheapness or lack of skilled labor, most coving gouges are brutally stamped out by machine, which, at best, can produce only a half circle. At worst the underside of the tool has two almost straight sides, two corners and a semi-circular bottom. Imagine this doing a smooth full roll on a rest! It is well worth the time to remedy these defects by grinding—it would be exceedingly difficult to make them worse. Again, the blade of the gouge is not likely to be the ideal shape. Common faults are a second bevel at the tip, a flattened cutting edge, the top not nearly rounded over, leaving corners, (the term "lady's fingernail" is very descriptive of the proper shape), and often the bevel is not long enough.

Unlike the roughing-down gouge, which always has a 45° bevel, the bevels of coving gouges can be varied to suit the user, although they must not be too short. As a guideline, measure the breadth of the bevel of the roughing-down gouge, and at least double this for the coving gouges. The bevel of the ¼-in. gouge will perform better if it is longer than that of the ¾-in. gouge.

Begin grinding with the blade on the rest, flute up, with the point of the gouge in the middle and just clear of the stone. Unlike grinding the roughing-down gouge, it is not good enough just to roll the blade from side to side because this operation would soon remove the point. The handle must be lowered as the blade is rolled to the left, so the extreme left-hand corner rides up to the same height that the point was when the operation started. The movement is then reversed, raising the handle as the point rolls onto the stone and lowering it as the right-hand edge comes around. A beginner should try some dry runs on a motionless stone, experimenting by look and feel with the movement needed to grind the bevel evenly. I keep the handle straight up and down during the whole operation. A beginner might find it easier to move the handle slightly from side to side, although I don't think the bevel can ever be ground as evenly this way. Again, the grinding need not be continued right to the edge. The safer but more laborious method of hand-honing can finish it off.

Roughing down a cylinder

Any piece of wood about 10 in. long and from 2 in. to 3 in. square with lengthwise grain will do for practice in roughing down a cylinder. Unseasoned wood of medium hardness will cut more easily and show the beginner if he is using the tools correctly. Mount the wood between centers and adjust the tool rest at a height just below center line and about ⅛ in. clear of the corners, testing this by rotating the wood by hand. Lathe speed should be anywhere between 1,000 and 2,000 rpm. Place a lamp at the back of the lathe so that it shines on the work but not in your eyes.

To rough from square to round: Lift the handle until the edge contacts the blur, traverse from left to right and roll the gouge.

End of first cut; small chips are 'corners' wood. Now go back again, slowly rolling the gouge, handle always lower than cutting edge.

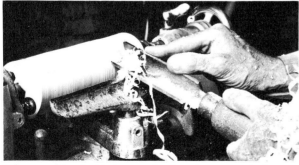

When wood is cylindrical, gouge produces long, even shavings.

Start the lathe and stand back. You will see a distinct round shape, surrounded by a blurred border. The blur is the corners of the wood, which progressively have to be removed. Place the 1¼-in. gouge on the center of the rest, handle lower than the blade, flute directly uppermost, edge above and just away from the work. The left hand (assuming a right-handed turner) should be over the flute, holding the blade quite firmly down on the rest. Lift the handle until the edge contacts the blur. There should be only a slight jolt. Working from either direction, take the gouge along the rest to the end and back again, removing small chips of wood on the way. The chips will increase in size as the work progresses, until a cylinder shape results. Do not concentrate the gaze on the tool edge all the time—when you feel it is cutting properly, look at the top of the revolving wood, where you should actually see the cutting action. You can stop the lathe at intervals to see what is happening, or without stopping, trail the finger tips lightly over and around the back of the turning wood. Any slight irregularity means it is not circular at that point.

Stop the lathe when the wood is a cylinder. Don't worry now about exactness of size all along the length. At this stage you can demonstrate to yourself in safe, slow motion the correct cutting, not scraping, action of the gouge. Place the gouge on the rest, flute facing upwards with the heel of the bevel touching the wood. This means that the handle will be held well down from the horizontal and the actual cutting edge will be just clear of the wood. Have the lathe turned slowly by hand. The blade will be in contact with the wood, just rubbing it lightly. Move the gouge slowly along, and at the same time gradually lift up the handle. When the angle of cut is correct, the edge will start to remove a thin shaving and the bevel will be in full contact with the wood surface. If the handle is lifted too high, the bevel will leave the wood, the cutting action will stop, and the resultant scrape of the edge will not only remove wood in a most unsatisfactory manner but will also immediately blunt the sharpest of edges.

Working with the flute facing fully upwards all the time is not a good idea, because only the center of the edge is cutting. The whole edge has been sharpened and so it all can be used—roll the gouge as it travels along the rest. The 1¼-in. gouge is a powerful tool that can remove large quantities of wood in a hurry. Unlike the bowl gouge, it has no ugly tendencies. If the butt of the handle is braced on the hip and the legs splayed, the blade can be swung from end to end by sideways movement of the hips. The body powers the cut, the hands control it.

Long slow curves are easy with the 1¼-in. gouge. Cut with light pressure, starting from the extreme left end of the wood, then roll gradually towards the middle, increasing pressure and thereby removing more wood at the center. Stop, and repeat the cut from the right side towards the center. Watch the top of the wood while cutting, because this helps keep the curves smooth.

For surface smoothing hold the gouge down on the rest with the flute over on either side. Bring the handle up until the blade starts cutting. Don't roll the blade, but watch the top of the wood and take smoothing cuts by pulling or pushing the blade along the rest.

Some economists think they can take a large-size heavy-duty pointed-nose coving gouge with a shallow flute, grind the nose square, and use it in place of a deep-throated roughing-down gouge. This does not work nearly as well.

Cutting coves, hollows and balls

Imagine a large capital "S" standing upright as in normal print. Lean it over to the right at an angle of 45°. Gouges can make the "ball shape" (top of the "S") and the hollow (middle and tail). It is impossible to cut the cove at the tail of the "S" in one operation, because after cutting halfway the gouge would be forced uphill. Coves can be scraped uphill, but no amount of abrasive paper will eliminate the damage caused to the wood fibers.

To form coves, make a cylinder between centers, about 2 in. in diameter and of any length. Use a pencil on the rest, and with the wood revolving, mark a line, then another one not more than ¾ in. away from the first, and not less than ⅝ in. Pick a ½-in. spindle gouge, and with the flute on the left side of the rest, try to enter the point into the line on the right. Unless you are lucky, the gouge will skid along the rest to your right. Until the point of the gouge has penetrated the wood there is no back-up support from any part of the bevel. The turning wood rejects the gouge and makes it skid.

Position the tool rest below center height so that with the gouge held completely horizontally, on its side, flute facing

To start a cove, hold the gouge firmly and push its point in slowly.

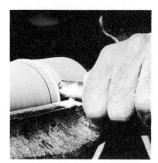

Remove half the waste in one cut by pushing firmly in and rolling the gouge onto its back. Right, the finished cove.

left, the point of the gouge is pointing directly at the right-hand line and in a position to make contact at center height of the wood. Push the point forward so that it is just in contact with the wood and hold it there, rubbing the surface. Holding very firmly, push the point in slowly. Only very little penetration is needed—1/16 in. is too much. Once some penetration has been achieved without skid, the danger is all over. If you still cannot manage it, remove the skid marks and make small notch marks with a parting tool instead of pencil lines, then proceed. Now, holding firmly down on the rest, push straight into the wood while twisting the gouge so that it is turning over on its back (flute ends up facing upwards), removing, quite brutally, half the waste wood towards the left. Try to remove this half in one attempt. Otherwise you will leave a "collar" of waste in the center of the cove.

Repeat from the left-hand line and remove the other half of the wood. If you find you do leave a collar, you are not taking out enough waste with the two cuts, or else you are trying to do too large a cove with too small a gouge. The result of these two scooping cuts does not look pretty, but the cutting actions that follow clean it all up nicely.

Using the right-hand side of the cove again, present the blade, flute facing left, with the point at the position at which the cut has to start. Keep just inside the rough-cut beginning—otherwise you will skid away again. Keeping the bevel just slightly away from the wood will enable you to put the point in and start the cut. The handle will be just down from the horizontal and a little over to the left. The full cut is completed by swinging the handle over to the right (thereby bringing the bevel into contact) and proceeding down the right-hand slope, gradually rolling the gouge over on its back

To start a ball shape, rub the bevel on the line, roll the gouge and lift the handle. Start each successive cut a little closer to the center line, but don't move the tool along the rest during any one cut.

(flute up) to finish at the bottom of the cove. Do not go past center of bottom. Sometimes I will allow just a little way past so that this area cleans up nicely without ridging.

Reverse the directions and cut down from the left-hand line. If you do not attempt heavy cuts you can do these alternate ones nice and slowly, watching and feeling the cut working properly. Alternate cuts from side to side will deepen and shape the cove to your satisfaction.

The coving gouge, which many beginners think is just for hollows, can also form quite attractive ball shapes. Right at the full diameter it cannot finish as cleanly as the skew chisel or the beading and parting tool, but it can get quite near.

Make the usual practice cylinder, 2 in. in diameter between centers. Somewhere along cut down a groove to about ½-in. in diameter. To give room for the gouge to work, widen it to 1 in. in length. Repeat the process 2 in. away so that you are left with a 2-in. block with room to work at either side. Pencil a line around the center of the block. Then pencil two more so that the wood has three equidistant lines running around it. We will start work from left to right.

With the lathe stopped place the gouge on the wood with the point upwards at the right-hand line, the bevel straddling the line, and the flute up. Turn the lathe slowly by hand. Keeping the blade on the rest and at a right angle to the wood, slide the blade down the wood, keeping the bevel rubbing, until the point takes hold and starts a small cut. Keep this going by gradually twisting the blade over to the right while progressively raising the handle. This action continues until the corner of the block has become slightly rounded and the gouge comes off the cut. You will find that the gouge has to be rolled and the handle lifted a surprising distance to accomplish such a short area of cut.

Start the lathe and do a similar cut, increasing the rounded area. Do another with the lathe stopped, slowly so that you can feel how much more freedom and lift you have to give the tool to keep it going over each full cut. Then you can gradually progress back to the block's center line, increasing the rounded area down to the ½-in. short spindle. You are cutting from large diameter to small with the bevel rubbing all the time. Down at the ½-in. spindle, the gouge will have been rolled over so much in order to keep it cutting that the flute finally ends up facing completely right.

Ensure that whatever hand is on the rest does not move along at all during any one cut. Keep your tool bevels at the correct length, hollow ground or dead flat, and sharpen often. And above all, do not try to cut wood uphill. □

Q & A

Production spindle turning—*I need to turn 200 maple handles, and may need another batch in the future. Do you have any tips for short-run production of spindle turnings? I don't want to invest in any automatic gadgets for my lathe.* —Robert Howe, Bennington, Vt.

MAC CAMPBELL REPLIES: To begin with, make sure your lathe has enough power—1 HP minimum for production work. If possible, get a ball-bearing tailstock center and buy or make a tool rest at least as long as the spindles you'll be turning. I made up 18-in. and 24-in. rests from angle iron.

Most of your regular tools are okay, but get a *big* roughing gouge. The extra mass is steadier, dissipates heat better, virtually eliminates vibration, and is easier and faster to use. I had a blacksmith make mine from a piece of 3-in. by ⅜-in. thick truck leaf spring. It has the usual U-shaped section, but straighter wings than most roughing gouges. The blade is 14 in. long, and the 1½-in. dia. handle is 16 in. long.

A duplicating gauge will prove really handy. It's a bar that mounts behind the work, parallel to it. On the bar is a series of fingers that rest against the spinning stock. You set each finger to the diameter you want, and when you've reached it, the finger has nothing to rest on anymore and drops past the turning. You can buy the gauge at Sears for about $50 (1984 price), or you can make one yourself.

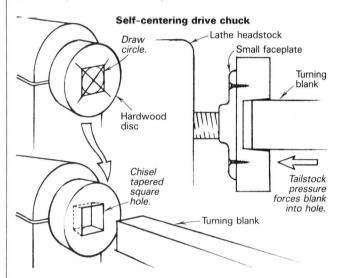

Self-centering drive chuck

Draw circle.

Lathe headstock

Small faceplate

Turning blank

Hardwood disc

Chisel tapered square hole.

Tailstock pressure forces blank into hole.

Turning blank

You'll need a self-centering drive chuck. On a small faceplate, mount a hardwood disc about 4 in. in diameter and 1 in. thick. With the lathe turning, mark a circle near the center of the disc with a pencil. If your turning blanks will be, say, 1½ in. square, mark a 1½-in. dia. circle. Remove the disc from the faceplate and, using the circle as a guide, chisel a square hole almost all the way through the wood, making it (for a 1½-in. square turning blank) just slightly larger than 1½ in. at the top, tapering to just under 1½ in. at the bottom. Remount the wood on the faceplate and leave it there.

Cut your turning blanks uniformly, and center-punch one end of each blank for the tailstock. I keep a punch ground to match the taper of my ball-bearing tailstock.

For future production runs of the same piece, you'll need a set-up pattern. Rough-turn a handle close to, but just shy of, final dimensions to allow room for smoothing. With the handle still on the lathe, adjust the fingers of the duplicating gauge so they fall just past the turning. Mark the locations of the fingers by holding a pencil against the rotating blank and remove it from the lathe. With this pattern you can reposition the gauge fingers for future production runs.

Sanding and Finishing on the Lathe

by David Ward

The first step to a good finish is a good sanding job: beginning with a coarse grit and not skipping grits. Sanding lathe work involves unique problems because it is impossible to sand with the grain while the lathe is running. Consequently, a lot of time is spent removing cross-grain scratches.

This problem can be solved on convex surfaces by using an orbital sander. With a sander, the grit does not remain in one place long enough to create scratches. Another advantage of an or-bital sander is that it won't dip into soft spots in the grain the way hand-held sandpaper will. The technique works so well that in sanding decayed wood, the edge of a void can become too sharp and need softening by hand, with 320 grit or so. Areas of the turning not accessible with the sander can be reached with strips of sandpaper reinforced with clear Mylar packing tape.

I don't have any magic answers for sanding inside surfaces, but the process can be made less painful by spraying sheets of sandpaper with pressure-sensitive adhesive (3M's #75) and sticking them together back to back. Tear off pieces, and the grit on one side keeps the sandpaper from slipping off the finger while the other side sands.

Another technique that I find essential in achieving a good sanding job is something I call flip-flopping—spinning the piece in one direction and then in the other while sanding. Wood fibers tend to bend over rather than being cut off, especially on end grain. Reversing the lathe bends them back and forth until they are cut off. (See p. 19 for suggestions for installing a reversing switch.) Be sure the faceplate is tightened securely before trying this.

Once the piece is adequately sanded I use a finishing process that is a takeoff on French polishing. The ingredients are similar and so are the results, but the method of application is much different. The turning is first soaked with raw linseed oil. This brings out the color of wood better than any other oil or mixture I've tried. After a few minutes, wipe off the excess oil and apply liberally a mixture of about 25 parts orange or white shellac and 1 part raw linseed oil. The oil lubricates the finish when it is being buffed. Too little oil will cause the surface to drag, while too much will not permit the shellac to heat up enough. The proportions may need adjusting for a specific application.

After the shellac-and-oil mixture has dried for two to ten minutes, depending on how porous the wood is, run the lathe at a fairly high speed. Step to one side before doing so, however, to avoid a shower. Then hold a pad of folded soft cotton cloth firmly against the turning. Most of the excess shellac will be quickly removed, leaving a clear surface on the work. The surface must be burnished with increasing pressure until the finish ceases to migrate, as observed in the glare of a light. At this point any shellac remaining on the wood has been driven into the wood by heat and pressure.

I usually apply a final coat of clear shoe wax for extra luster and durability. The end result is a hard surface finish that does not coat the wood with plastic—a penetrating finish that will not dull with time and takes minutes rather than hours to complete. This finish works well on most hardwoods. □

David Ward is a turner in Glenwood Springs, Colo.

Photos: David Plush

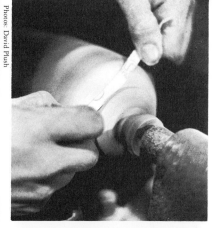

Author sands turning with orbital sander, above, which eliminates cross-grain scratches and does not dip into soft areas of grain, as does hand-held sandpaper. A thin strip of sandpaper backed with Mylar tape, above right, reaches places where the sander will not go. Turnings can be 'French polished,' right, by applying a shellac-and-oil mixture and rubbing it out with the lathe at high speed until the mixture has been driven into the wood.

The Taming of the Skew
Subtlety, not force, wins favor

by Mike Darlow

For each piece of wood, an efficient turner employs the minimum number of tools, each, if possible, only once. This means being able to use each tool for a variety of cuts. No tool in a turner's kit has greater potential for this than the skew chisel—it planes surfaces smooth, cuts balls and beads, defines fillets and even makes coves, working all the while with a precise, responsive touch—yet the skew has a reputation for being the most unforgiving and unpredictable turning tool. It requires large, confident movements to slice its thin shavings, but a single small movement in the wrong direction can cause the tool to dig in and ruin the work. Indeed, the *Fine Woodworking Design Books* confirm, to my eye, that many turners deliberately avoid cuts requiring the skew, compromising on the preferred design in order to be able to use a gouge or scraper. If you slice with a skew instead of scraping, you will cut cleaner and produce finished work faster. We can create confidence in the skew by understanding the tool's geometry and practicing the various cuts.

Tool geometry—The skew is a long, straight-bladed chisel with its cutting edge ground at an angle to produce two very different points—an acute one called the long point, and an obtuse one called the short point (figure 1). There are two bevels, usually equal, ground on the sides of the tool to form the cutting edge. Perpendicular to the sides are two edges: one

leading to the long point, called the long edge, and one leading to the short point, called the short edge.

For consistency, it is essential that the skew's sides are truly parallel, so that the cutting edge can be parallel to both of them, and that the long and short edges are at 90° to the sides. The width of the sides defines the nominal size of the skew, and sizes vary between ¼ in. and 2 in. Most general turning is done using a ¾-in. or 1-in. skew. This is a compromise between a long cutting edge (an advantage in planing) and narrow sides (which allow work in tight places). If a constricted space dictates using a smaller tool for part of the work, a production turner must decide whether to use a small skew for the whole job, or to pick up two or more different skews. If there is a large proportion of planing in the work, the turner will probably use two. Where a skew with sides narrower than ¼ in. is required, it is preferable to grind the long edge down at the end to make a shorter cutting edge in order to preserve reasonable stiffness. The minimum thickness of a skew should be ¼ in., or else the tool will be flexible and hence dangerous.

An important advantage of the skewed cutting edge is that this skewness provides a clearance angle for making certain cuts. When the tool is correctly shaped and sharpened, you can make the finishing cut on a shoulder, for instance, without the skew digging in. Set the skew's long edge flat on the

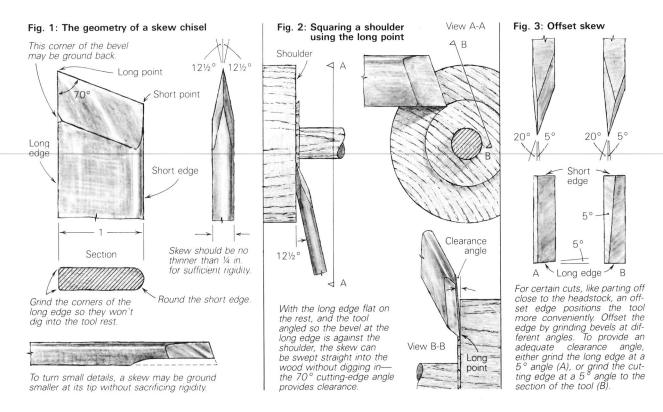

Fig. 1: The geometry of a skew chisel

This corner of the bevel may be ground back.

Long point — 70° — Short point

12½° 12½°

Long edge — Short edge

1 — Section

Skew should be no thinner than ¼ in. for sufficient rigidity.

Grind the corners of the long edge so they won't dig into the tool rest.

Round the short edge.

To turn small details, a skew may be ground smaller at its tip without sacrificing rigidity.

Fig. 2: Squaring a shoulder using the long point

Shoulder — A

12½° — A

With the long edge flat on the rest, and the tool angled so the bevel at the long edge is against the shoulder, the skew can be swept straight into the wood without digging in—the 70° cutting-edge angle provides clearance.

View A-A — B

B

Clearance angle

View B-B — Long point

Fig. 3: Offset skew

20° 5° — 20° 5°

Short edge

5°

5°

A — Long edge — B

For certain cuts, like parting off close to the headstock, an offset edge positions the tool more conveniently. Offset the edge by grinding bevels at different angles. To provide an adequate clearance angle, either grind the long edge at a 5° angle (A), or grind the cutting edge at a 5° angle to the section of the tool (B).

From *Fine Woodworking* magazine (September 1982) 36:70-75

tool rest with the left-hand bevel at right angles to the lathe axis (figure 2), and push the skew straight in—the clearance angle makes the cut both easy and safe. Good turning is based upon confidence which is, in turn, based upon your tool's being predictable. The clearance angle is only about 5°, and hence if the tool is incorrectly shaped or sharpened the clearance angle may be larger on one side and smaller on the other, and predictability is lost.

In use, a side or an edge of the skew must always be in contact with the tool rest. To facilitate smooth movements over the rest, it helps to grind the short edge of the skew slightly convex, and to round the corners of the long edge. The tool rest and the sides of the tool should be smooth.

Sharpening—An angle of skewness of about 70° is the optimum compromise between retaining a strong long point and providing an adequate clearance angle. When grinding, hold the cutting edge parallel to the grinding wheel axis, the bevel flat on the wheel, and aim for an angle on each bevel of about 12½°, as shown in figure 1. I find that this sharpening angle works well on all woods, even our native Australian hardwoods (some of which are very hard indeed). The optimum diameter of the grindstone is 8 in. to 10 in. If smaller, excessive hollow grinding weakens the cutting edge; if larger, the bevel will be rather flat, which makes both grinding and honing more difficult. The grit and composition of the wheel depend on the type of steel. For my high-speed steel tools, I use a Norton 19A 60KVBE. Take care to keep the two bevels the same length, so that the cutting edge, when looked at head-on, is centered and parallel to the sides. Then the clearance angle will be the same on both sides.

There are two misconceptions about sharpening: that the bevel need not be hollow-ground, and that honing is not required after grinding. The bevels need to be hollow-ground so that there is a straight line of sight along the bevel. The turner can then sight along the true cutting edge, the microsharpened bevel, when making cuts with the long point. Although gouges are more easily honed by moving the stone over the tool, I prefer to use a fixed stone for the skew. Try a shallow tray holding a fine-grade 6-in. by 2-in. oilstone immersed in kerosene, plus the slips for the gouges, mounted adjacent to the lathe and covered with a lid. Hone the skew with short to-and-fro strokes, and with both the heel and the toe of the bevel bearing on the stone. After both bevels have been honed, any burr can be stropped off.

25° — Microsharpened bevel
Flat-honed surface
Hollow-ground section (curvature exaggerated)
Flat-honed surface
Line of sight

Some turners do not hone, perhaps because the ragged edge straight from the grindstone gives an illusion of sharpness. An unhoned edge, however, scratches the wood surface and does not last. In addition, it is far quicker to rehone than to regrind, and your tools will last much longer.

A convex bevel is occasionally recommended in the belief that it polishes the cut surface. Actually, the texture of the wood contacted by the bevel is little affected by bevel shape, and the loss of the clear line of sight is a disadvantage.

Steel—Almost all ready-made turning tools are carbon tool steel, as it is easier for the manufacturers to fabricate. Here, in

A pencil gauge is used to mark a roughed-out cylinder. A shallow groove in the plywood supports the pencil point, allowing the turner to precisely transfer marks to the spinning work.

Australia, professionals usually use high-speed steel—it takes a finer edge, is more resistant to abrasion and does not lose its temper as readily as carbon tool steel does. It is especially recommended for the skew chisel with its exposed long point, which overheats easily. The amateur can change to high-speed steel by making his own long-and-strong skews. Hardened and tempered rectangular tool bits about 1 ft. long need only to have the bevels and tang ground by the turner himself. Of the vast range of tool steels available, American Iron & Steel Institute classifications T1 and M1 are best, being the least brittle of the true high-speed steels. Sears sells high-speed steel turning tools at a reasonable price, but the blades are shorter than I like.

Handles—The skew should be worked with a sensitive touch, not brute force. On spindle turning the skew will usually be used for most of the turning time, and it will go through many complex movements. For good balance and leverage, the overall length should be about 18 in., and the handle should be light and fairly short rather than long and heavy. It's less tiring and gives better balance when you use the tool one-handed. My 12-in. tool blanks allow me to make long-and-strong tools with a 9-in. blade showing and a 9-in. handle. Although a rack of tools with matched handles looks very smart, having them all different, both in shape and wood, helps you find one fast when you want it.

Laying out the cuts—To turn a few identical items, I begin with a roughing gouge (deep, U-shaped flute ground straight across; no pointed nose) to remove the bulk of the wood. A truly sharp one will leave the surface ready for marking out and detailed turning. Then I use a pencil gauge (photo above). The gauge is ¼ in. to ½ in. thick, about 3 in. wide, and usually about 1 in. longer than the work. Draw the pattern full-size on the gauge, and project the main reference points to the edge. File short grooves where the lines meet the edge of the gauge. To mark out, rest the gauge on the tool rest with its top edge lightly touching the rotating wood, and hold a pencil point against the turning at the grooves.

A conventional turning has several features, as shown in figure 4. A bead, an approximately semicircular convex curve, frequently ends at a short fillet forming a break between the bottom of the bead and a cove. A bead turned on a long curve is called a ring. Some spindle turning requires only a roughing gouge, a skew and a detail gouge, each being used only once during the process. Here are some of the cuts that can be made with the skew, roughly in the order in which they might be used.

V-cuts—To turn a bead, there must be clearance for the skew to move into and for the shavings to escape. The V-cut, with the skew resting on its long edge, is the first clearing cut. It spears into the wood, leading with the long point. To begin cutting a bead, three V-cuts are usually necessary. For the first, hold the tool at right angles to the lathe axis, with its

Fig. 4: A typical turning

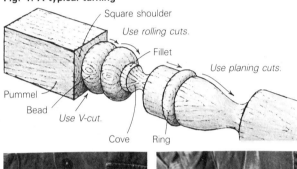

Square shoulder
Use rolling cuts.
Fillet
Use planing cuts.
Pummel
Bead
Use V-cut.
Cove   Ring

Left, the third V-cut: Move the tool laterally to the right, then swing and rotate the handle so the cutting edge points along the intended line of cut. Sweep the point down to make the cut. To leave a pummel (right), cut the shoulder before the stock is roughed out. Make a series of V-cuts to achieve enough depth, then align the bevel at the skew's long point with the shoulder. With the long edge flat on the rest, arc the skew into the work, taking a light cut. The skew's built-in clearance angle makes the cut safe and easy.

long edge on the tool rest, and position the long point above the mark for the outer edge of the bead. Raise the handle so the point sweeps down into the wood. This initial cut is admittedly crude—the skew's tip crushes the wood on each side of the bevel, resulting in considerable friction and heat. There is little metal at the long point, so heat is only slowly conducted away into the body of the blade. Too heavy and sustained a pressure will create temperatures at the tool tip that are high enough to soften carbon steel. The two succeeding V-cuts widen and, where necessary, deepen the groove. Move the skew a little to the side of the first cut. Swing and rotate the handle so that the cutting edge points at the bottom of the first cut. Then raise the handle so that the long point sweeps down in an arc until it reaches the bottom of the first cut, as shown in the photo, bottom left. The process can be repeated, deepening and widening the V until sufficient depth is reached.

To leave a square, or pummel, on a turned piece, the procedure is similar, although the V-cutting precedes roughing. Obviously, because of the greater depth of wood at the corners, more than three V-cuts are usually required. Make alternate perpendicular and sloping cuts until the shoulder is deep enough. These initial V-cuts leave a rough surface, so a final, light V-cut should be taken down the face of the square to the full finished depth. At the long point itself, the bevel facing the square should be at right angles to the lathe axis, which requires that you swing the handle slightly, as shown in the photo, bottom right. As long as the long edge is flat on the tool rest, you will come to no harm.

In cutting a bead, V-cuts define both the bead's lateral extent and, more important, its depth. After the V-cuts have angled in to clear room, the short point can make a series of rolling cuts to shape the curve. On stock of the size in the photos on the facing page, cutting each side of a bead usually requires three V-cuts followed by at least two rolling cuts.

Rolling cuts—In bead-cutting, use the very end of the cutting edge at the short point. The cut starts with the skew almost flat on its side. Hence to start a rolling cut, the handle must be rotated to tilt the cutting edge slightly so only the short point cuts. Also, the handle must be angled slightly behind the cut so that the cutting edge, not the short edge, is presented to the wood, as shown in the top photo and the bottom left photo on the facing page. Then, as shown in the middle photo, simultaneously rotate the short point to take a deeper cut, and—to keep the cutting edge in the work—move it around the side of the bead and vertically downward. It is often necessary to slide the blade along the rest. This involves quite large movements of the handle, swinging through a wide lateral arc and rising steadily, in order to keep the bevel rubbing and the short point cutting.

The underhand turning grip, visible in the photo at the top of the next page, makes control easier than conventional overhand grips. In this grip, which is widely used in Australia, the forefinger of the left hand extends under the tool rest and is used to steady the hand and power the tool. Left hand, tool and tool rest are tied together and can act as a unit. Provided that there is a gap of at least ½ in. between the work and the tool rest, the finger is safe.

To achieve a full semicircular bead at the end of the rolling cut, the skew has to cut perpendicularly to the lathe axis. Unfortunately, the clearance angle—of such assistance when

To begin a full rolling cut with the short point, start at the top of the bead with the skew almost on its side. Angle the handle slightly behind the cut to keep the cutting edge, not the short edge, in contact with the wood. When making rolling cuts, Darlow uses the Australian underhand grip, his forefinger gripping the back of the tool rest for better control.

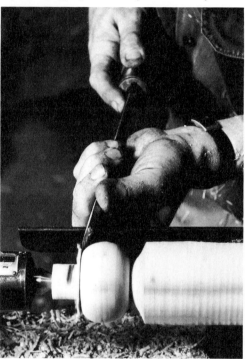
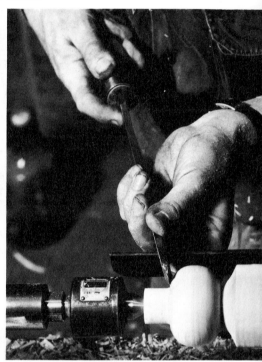

Almost flat on its side, the short point begins to cut (left). Move the skew laterally along the tool rest to continue (center), rotating the handle to keep the overhanging cutting edge clear. Keep your elbows near your body for better control, swinging your body to pivot the skew on the tool rest. Raise the handle and move the

cutting edge down into the work to keep the short point cutting. At the completion of the cut (right), the handle is rising and moving forward—Darlow has swung it far to the right with his body and rotated it so that the cutting edge, beyond the vertical, can form the side of the bead perpendicular to the work.

you are using the long point—becomes an interference angle when you are using the short point. Therefore, at the end of the cut the handle must be rotated so the blade tilts about 5° away from the cut, as shown in the photo at far right. This is why it helps to round the short edge of the skew, so that there is no sudden change in the cutting edge's relationship to the work when you transfer from one fulcrum to the other.

There are three main problems when making rolling cuts. First, if you fail to rotate the handle enough as you move around the bead, the overhanging part of the cutting edge will bite into the part of the bead you have just cut. This causes the working length of the cutting edge to increase suddenly from virtually nil to up to perhaps ¼ in. The cutting force increases almost instantaneously. Human reaction time is too slow to keep control of the tool, and it is shoved back, riding up and out of the bead. Second, if you inadvertently take too thick a shaving—by raising the handle too far, swinging it too soon around the bead or rotating it excessive-

ly—the strong shaving formed outside the short point will force the cutting tip farther into the side of the bead, ruining the shape. Third, if you persist in using a dull tool, it will not be able to penetrate the wood at the correct working angle—the tool will ride on top, compressing and glazing the surface, and making penetration even more difficult. When you try to get below the burnished surface, the tool will dig in. There is no cure except to sharpen your skew.

Rolling cuts are the main cause for the skew's notoriety. They require simultaneous lateral, vertical and rotational movements of the cutting point, plus lateral movement of the blade along the rest to make smooth curves without digging in. Needless to say, they need to be taken slowly, and they require considerable practice so that they become almost automatic. A bead of about ½-in. diameter is a good size to practice. It rolls naturally without the necessity of moving the skew laterally along the rest, although the handle still rises and swings through its broad arc, and the tool must be guid-

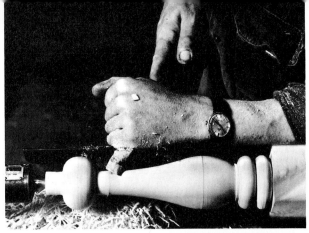

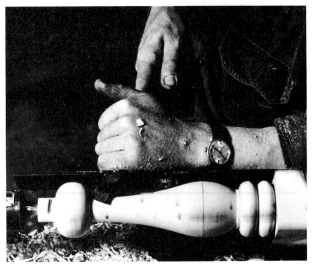

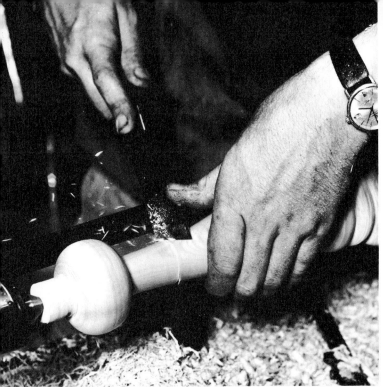

The planing cut, with the bevel rubbing the work to support the cutting edge, leaves a smooth, polished surface. Darlow guides the skew with his thumb while his left hand dampens vibration in slender stock, above. Generally, as shown at top right, neither the short point nor the long point should contact the work. The bottom right photo shows a modification: the slide cut, a planing cut that gradually leads up to using the extreme short point to cut the end of a curve without marring the side of a bead. As in all turning where most of the tool movement is horizontal, the conventional overhand grip is used.

ed forward over its pivot point on the rest. Larger sizes, with full rolling cuts, are less automatic and more difficult to learn. Many turners favor several short, overlapping rolling cuts, with the sideways movements in between.

When practicing, do not attempt too much at once and do not practice when you are tired or when things begin to go badly. Take a rest to restore your concentration. Don't use too large a square at first, 2 in. to 3 in. is about right. Use a gouge to clean up any scars on the work before proceeding or you may dig in again in the same place.

In the series of rolling cuts necessary to complete a bead, you are aiming for a constant shaving thickness. The cuts should be taken slowly and purposefully so that all the varying movements can be coordinated. There is also the problem of whether to watch the skew's cutting tip or the evolving bead profile. Obviously it is best to watch both simultaneously, but for those without Eddie Cantor's optical facility, watch the tip initially, and once the cut is started, switch to the profile. When you are comfortable making full rolling cuts with the short point, you will have few problems with the rest of the skew's repertoire. Here are some tips on the other cuts.

Long-point cuts—Most beads can be cut with either the long or the short point. The short point works better. It cuts down into the wood, thus burnishing the surface, whereas the long point lifts the ends of the wood fibers, so an inferior, almost porous surface is left. In addition, because the microsharpened bevel at the short point is supported by the work, there is less tendency for a jerky rolling action than when you are using the relatively unsupported long point. But do use the long point for very small beads, where the greater visibil-

ity helps. Ideally, you should execute the cut the same as you would with the short point, starting with the skew on its side and rotating the cutting edge through a full 90° until the blade rests on its long edge.

Where you cannot lay the blade on its side to start the rolling cut—as on the far side of a bead adjacent to a square section, where the corners of the square would hit the skew—you can use the long point, held more vertically, to make a series of rounded V-cuts to define the bead. Alternatively, and this means a time-consuming tool change, a very small skew or a nosed gouge could be used for a better surface.

When similar beads are adjacent, it is not possible to rotate the skew far enough to make the bead bottoms truly vertical. Cut as close to vertical as you can, until the skew begins to bind, then reach in with the long point to cut out any rags left in the cusp.

Cutting fillets—After completing the shape of the bead, and clearing some room, cut the fillet using the short point. As with the start of a rolling cut, angle the handle away slightly to present the short point of the cutting edge to the wood. It is easiest to keep the tool at one point on the tool rest, and to swing the handle so the cutting point levels the fillet. Don't contact, and hence spoil, the side of the bead above the fillet. Normally, fillets are cut parallel to the lathe's axis, although where room is constricted they are often sloped to avoid having to switch to a narrow skew.

Planing cuts—The planing cut, shown in the photos above, is a finishing cut that leaves curved and straight sections smooth and even. It consists of mostly lateral motion of the skew along the tool rest. The planing cut is made with the short point leading, the supporting bevel almost tangential to the surface, and the cut always moving level or downhill. The cutting edge usually works at about 45° to the lathe axis, giving both a cutting and a riving action. The full length of the cutting edge can be used, with the exception of the long and short points themselves. The larger the diameter of the work, the larger the skew that should be used, in order to keep the points safely away from the work. If the long point becomes buried, the shaving is cut only on its near side. The shaving thus offers more resistance, and pushes the long point down into the wood, resulting in a deep tear. If only the short point is cutting, the action becomes purely riving, and splinters, not shavings, will result.

Sensitive control, which is one of the joys of using the skew, is accomplished by slightly varying the presentation of the tool to the work. The movements, in various combinations, become so ingrained that they seem instinctive: To take a deeper cut, merely raise the handle. To increase the downhill gradient of the cut, slightly steepen the angle of the cutting edge by rotating the handle. Raising the tool rest for the planing cut is unnecessary and time-consuming. Simply lower the handle so that the tool is presented with the bevel supporting the cutting edge.

If you are planing thin work and encounter vibration that causes your skew to chatter, it is perfectly safe to support the work with your left hand as it turns. The photo at the left on the facing page shows me steadying a turning while I guide the skew along the cylinder with my thumb. Your left hand can also feel how successful the steadying is—if you've got it right, the turning will feel smooth.

The riving component of the cutting action causes tear-out on interlocked or non-axially grained wood unless the cuts happen to be fairly steeply downward. To minimize tearing out, angle the handle back behind the direction of travel so that the cutting edge is more nearly square—say, about 70°—to the lathe axis.

If you are doing work where the corner of the bevel at the long edge digs into the finished surface, you can grind the offending corner away, as shown in figure 1, or tilt the skew more steeply so the corner clears the work.

Where a long curve meets a ring or similar projection, modify the planing cut into what could be christened the slide cut. As you approach the projection with the skew planing, gradually slide the tool forward so that the short point itself cuts, as in the lower right photo on the facing page.

Planing cuts can define convex and concave profiles, as well as straight ones. Hollows with a surprisingly small radius can be cut with a skew, using a modified planing cut and firm control. The lower middle section of the cutting edge is used and the angle of the tool is somewhat steeper than the tangent at the point on the hollow being cut. With large work, control is difficult because the bevel is not supported, but with practice the technique will be found risk-free and safe. Use a small skew on work less than 1 in. in diameter. Always cut down toward the bottom of the cove from both sides—don't try to cut uphill.

Parting cuts—You can make V-cuts one-handed with the long point for parting off, which frees your other hand to steady and catch the finished turning. Slacken the tailstock a little toward the end of the cut so that the work will come

The skew can quickly remove waste. Keep the bevel rubbing, and the edge moving forward, as the diameter goes down. A firm grip is necessary.

away freely. Don't part off work too large to control or turnings with square sections at the left-hand end.

If you do much parting off from a chuck, you will want to be able to part off close to its face, which should be covered by a guard. The offset skew (figure 3) allows this, with its 5° right-hand bevel.

The skew can also set diameters and remove waste. Hold the cutting edge parallel to the lathe axis with the lower bevel rubbing, as in the photo above. The action is identical to that of the conventional parting tool—which should slice rather than scrape—except that the skew will tend to move sideways in the direction of its long point. You cannot make this cut, of course, unless there is clearance for the short edge of the tool. If holding the skew with only the right hand (the left hand holding the caliper), brace the handle beneath your forearm, extend your forefinger down the tool for firmness, and don't use a skew wider than ½ in.

Steering the skew—The right hand provides most of the power and steering. When doing a series of cuts with a particular tool, it is natural to regrip for each cut so that the right hand is comfortable during that cut. For rolling cuts, however, it is best to grip the tool so that the right hand reaches the natural, comfortable position at the completion of the cut. This makes the cut almost automatic because the right hand wants to return to an unstrained position.

Extending the forefinger, as I usually do, is a way of getting a more precise feel of the tool, as well as of adding firmness when needed. For control and balance, keep your right arm close to your side.

With any human activity, practice of the correct techniques, while perhaps not making perfect, at least makes much better. Unfortunately, new techniques tend to feel unnatural, so keep on turning and be prepared for things to get worse before they get better. □

Mike Darlow keeps four lathes busy turning lace bobbins, restorations, production work, bowls and gallery pieces in Chippendale, N.S.W., Australia. Photos by Peter Johnson, Sydney, Australia.

Movement and Support at the Lathe
A steady hold improves your turning

by Richard Raffan

Many aspiring turners experience problems because they fail to develop basic tool control. How you hold and move your tools, even how you stand at the lathe, affects the quality of your work. A solid, vibration-free lathe is of little use if an improperly held tool chatters about on the wood. In this article, I'll cover the basics—how to support yourself, the tool and the work—which are the same for all aspects of face or center work. Practice will greatly improve your technique.

Stance—When a tool contacts a spinning block of wood, the wood exerts considerable downward pressure on the cutting edge. Think of the tool as a lever and the tool rest as a fulcrum. When force is applied on the cutting end, there is an opposite reaction at the handle end. The farther the cutting edge is from the tool rest, the greater the leverage, and the more difficult it becomes to control the tool, so keep the rest as close to the wood as practicable.

To move the tool precisely where you want it, without the wood having a say in the matter, you must get your weight behind the tool. Stand in a balanced position, feet apart. Maintain contact between your body and the machine—keep a hand on the rest and lean against the lathe bed, or keep a leg against the stand. This gives you extra support and stability, and provides a point of reference for tool movement.

Keep the tool handle tight against your body or solidly braced against your forearm. With shorter, lighter tools, keep your elbows tucked into your sides, not moving about in the air. If the handle has to leave your side, align it solidly along your forearm. Your goal is a compact stance which, when combined with a firm grip, allows you to move the tool precisely with your weight behind it. Movement comes not so much from the wrists or arms, but from the shoulders, hips and legs. If you want to move the tool edge slightly left, then the movement comes from a shift of the hip to the right rather than from a hand movement. That way your hand stays close to your side and you're more compact. If you want the tool edge to drop, raise your whole side, standing on tiptoe if necessary, to bring the handle up, with the weight of your torso and shoulders behind the tool.

Lathe height is important. Block up the lathe or stand on boards so that the lathe center is about 50mm (2 in.) above your elbow. The height of the rest in relation to center height varies from one turning situation to another, but it should be close to center. Adjust the rest for comfort and try to keep the tool near horizontal.

Holding the tool—Hold the tool with the controlling hand (right hand if you're right-handed) somewhere on its handle. I grip the handle near its ferrule, because I find this more comfortable than holding it at the end, and I can use my forearm and body along the length of the handle to stabilize the tool. Gripping the tool this way, nearer the rest, also means that when I pivot the tool, my right hand need not move in quite so large an arc as it would if it were at the end of a long handle. Hold your upper hand (left hand if you're right-handed) on the rest near the cutting edge. This hand provides fine control. You must be able to control the tool at the point where it pivots on the rest if you are to dictate the precise path of the cutting edge. You can grip the tool from either above or below. Gripping from above gives firm support when you need to move the tool sideways along the rest, and by raising a few fingers, you can direct shavings away from your face. Gripping from below allows you to clamp tool and rest together to make a solid pivot point, while permitting you to watch the edge. No matter which grip you use, the object is the same: to keep hand and tool in contact

To get the most control, Raffan leans against the lathe, tool handle solidly against his side. His left hand assumes a hand-over grip—good for lateral movement along the rest.

with the rest, and to prevent the tool from moving sideways when you don't want it to.

Don't grip the tool as though your life depended on it. Just use a light, firm grip—relaxed, but ready to tighten instantly if necessary. This will provide a kind of recoil pad so that a catch will be less disastrous. It's possible to turn while holding the tool lightly between a finger and the thumb of your right hand. You have no fine control this way, but the trick illustrates how little power is required.

As your skill develops, you'll be able to adapt these grips to suit yourself. I enjoy the control I've gained through their application—moving the edge with a little squeeze or push here and there, in conjunction with broader movement from the rest of my body.

Cutting—Begin the cut with a firm grip on the tool, and always start above the center, or axis, of the wood. Don't push the tool straight across the rest into the wood—you get better control if you tilt the edge up 10° and bring it down in an arc by slowly raising the handle (figure 1).

I have three basic rules for cutting. First, whenever possible, cut the wood with the tool moving parallel to the lathe axis. This allows you to exert pressure in a direction where it will be absorbed by the headstock or tailstock (figure 2). Put as little forward pressure as possible against the axis of the wood, to avoid chatter. A sharp tool held in the optimum position will produce a large shaving with virtually no forward pressure against the wood. Experiment by rolling the tool to find this point.

Second, have the bevel of the gouge or chisel rubbing (which is impossible with any scraping technique.) This provides a secondary fulcrum and a guide to aid fine control of the tool's edge. Sometimes, when beginning a cut, this is not possible. In this case, use a firm-fulcrum grip, and move the tool into the wood through an arc. Then move the bevel so that it can rub the newly cut surface.

Third, avoid using the tools at right angles to the surface being cut. It is much more difficult to achieve flowing or straight lines this way. Hold the tool so that the edge is tangent to the work, and move the tool in the same direction as the curve (figure 3).

Learn to move the tool precisely and evenly along a definite path. Plan what you want to cut, and have a beginning, middle and end to your movements. Don't poke at the wood. Any shape poked at and messed about tends to look it, so make your cuts smooth, flowing and definite. The tool should move forward only after the wood in its path has been removed. In the hands of an expert, this becomes a rapid, flowing action.

Practice slowly. Don't try to cut too much at one go. If you push the tool in too fast, the sudden force will lead a catch. If the tool begins to cut less efficiently or stops cutting, adjust the tool angle and roll the tool to a different position. If you push forward to find an edge, the tool will often skate over

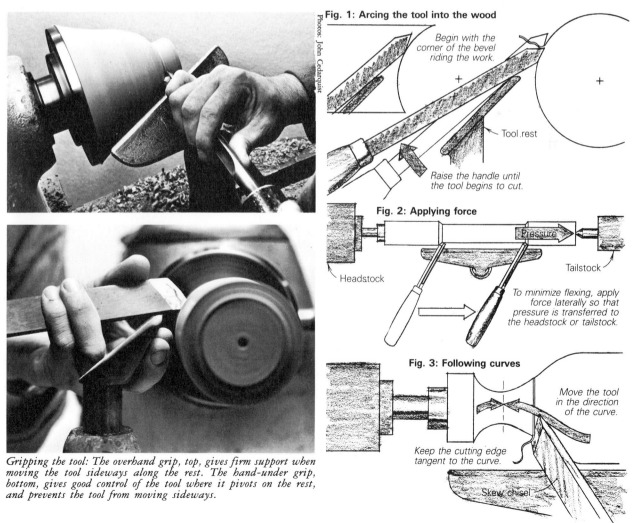

Fig. 1: Arcing the tool into the wood

Begin with the corner of the bevel riding the work.

Tool rest

Raise the handle until the tool begins to cut.

Fig. 2: Applying force

Pressure

Headstock

Tailstock

To minimize flexing, apply force laterally so that pressure is transferred to the headstock or tailstock.

Fig. 3: Following curves

Move the tool in the direction of the curve.

Keep the cutting edge tangent to the curve.

Skew chisel

Gripping the tool: The overhand grip, top, gives firm support when moving the tool sideways along the rest. The hand-under grip, bottom, gives good control of the tool where it pivots on the rest, and prevents the tool from moving sideways.

From *Fine Woodworking* magazine (January 1979) 44:40-42

Supporting the work: Any grip can be modified by extending fingers around the work to the back side to keep the wood from flexing (top left). Note how Raffan steadies his body on the lathe in the photo at left. To back up the thin wall of a bowl, above, Raffan uses his left-hand thumb to pin the tool to the rest, while the other fingers support the wood behind the cut.

the surface without cutting. The tool should never shoot forward if you lose an edge—that indicates a lack of control.

As a cut gets close to center, slow up for the last few millimeters and float the edge in gently, turning and adjusting the tool to maintain the most effective cut. Stop at dead center—don't cut below, or you risk tearing or pulling out fibers.

To improve your control, learn to stop in mid-cut. Practice easing pressure so that the edge of the tool is barely in contact with the wood. Then proceed again and stop again. Soon you should be able to remove the tool and bring it back to exactly the same position.

Practice and experience will teach you what each lathe tool can and can't do. If you have trouble, and don't know why, there are a few things to consider: First, check that the tool is sharp. If it is, but is still not cutting properly, experiment with different angles or roll the tool slightly. If this doesn't work, you may be using the wrong tool, so try another. If nothing seems to work, do some other job for a while, or go for a walk and try again later. Everyone has off days.

Supporting the wood—As you become more adventurous and turn slender pieces or bowls with thin walls, the wood will flex when a tool presses against it. If the wood flexes under power, it will vibrate, causing spiral chatter marks or worse. You'll hear a high, almost screeching sound if you're really overdoing it. You must support the wood. I always use my hand, which is far more flexible and sensitive than any mechanical support. One part supports the wood, while the other part remains in contact with the tool and rest. You can develop your own techniques, but your fingers or hand should support the wood from behind to provide counterpressure to the tool's pressure. If your hand gets hot, you're pushing too hard on the tool. Your hand should be warm, but not burning. Provide just enough support to keep the wood from flexing away from the center.

Sounds—Sounds are important in lathe work and you must learn them. Turning sounds should be a series of crescendos and decrescendos resulting from smooth, flowing cuts. Stop the lathe whenever you hear a new sound, to discover the cause. This is time-consuming at first, but you'll soon learn to recognize the basic noises—a sharp tool hisses; a dull tool makes a grinding sound. Once you hear the difference, it's easy to tell when your tool needs sharpening. With practice, you'll also be able to judge the thickness of a bowl wall, detect a loose block, or tell if you've hit a split or a knot, just by listening to the sound.

Attitude—It is worth pushing yourself. Don't be afraid to risk ruining a job with one chancey final cut. Sometimes just one more cut can make a lot of difference in the curve of a bowl. Once, when I checked the 8mm wall thickness of a large elm-burl bowl, I found it to be only 2.5mm thick near the base. I took a chance and turned the whole wall down to 2.5mm, and ended up with an even thickness—cut in one minute, not bludgeoned into submission with 20-grit abrasive in ten. That time I was successful. I've had smaller bowls shatter on me, but it is always worth the risk. Now and then you should cut bowls or boxes in half to examine the section. You can learn a great deal by doing this, and it's worth sacrificing some less-than-satisfactory pieces to help find out where you're going wrong.

As you develop your skills, beware of complacency. No matter how good you become, aspire to doing better. I find I am rarely satisfied with yesterday's masterpiece because it becomes today's run-of-the-mill. □

Richard Raffan, a professional turner, lives in Mittagong, N.S.W., Australia. His book Turning Wood with Richard Raffan *and the companion video of the same name are both available, separately or as a set, from The Taunton Press.*

Turning Tips

Advice from a mill man

by R. Perry Mercurio

Are you trying to sharpen your turning tools on a bench grinder with a wheel so hard and fine that the slightest touch of steel burns a blue spot of drawn temper? You can't turn without sharp tools and you can't keep them sharp that way. Find a mill supply house (most cities have at least one in the phone book) and let them help you select a good sharpening wheel. I'd suggest a Norton #32A60-J5VBE or a Universal-Simonds #RA60-J-V8 in a size to fit your grinder. These are soft wheels and should never be used for anything except sharpening hard steels. Your good wheel will last longer if you put a harder, general-purpose wheel on the other end of the grinder, and use it for rough work.

You won't get a good edge if your tools bounce around, so it's important to keep grinding wheels round and true and free of vibration. This is easily done with a star wheel or a diamond-tipped truing tool, or even with a piece of broken grinding wheel. The star wheel will give you the best surface.

If you don't have a regular grinder, you can make one by rigging up a stand, either of wood or of angle iron, whose top is a comfortable elbow height. Mount pillow blocks on the stand, then fix the grinding stones to the shaft and power it with a separate motor and V-belt.

Honing: There are as many ways of honing as there are stars in the sky, but my 40 years of mill experience has shown that the Crystolon pocket stone I bought for $1.19 plus a couple of hard Arkansas slip stones will do a very acceptable job. The pocket stone bites off the required amount of metal; the finer stone smooths and polishes. For these fine stones I'd suggest a Norton #HS-3, which has a tapered cross section with round edges, and a Norton #HF-843, which is diamond-shaped in section with sharp edges. These three stones will also do nearly all of your carving tools.

To touch up gouges, make a socket of some sort for the butt end of the handle, to steady it while you hone. Hold the tool firmly between your left thumb and fingers so you can rotate the gouge easily while stoning with your right hand.

To keep stones clean and free-cutting, keep them moist at all times. Make a shallow tray from the bottom of a large tin can. Put a few layers of cloth in the bottom, saturated with a mixture of half kerosene and half motor oil. Stones can't absorb too much oil, and it makes metal particles picked up by

R. Perry Mercurio, of Kingfield, Maine, is a retired plant engineer in the commercial woodturning industry.

the stone during honing loosen and shed. Hang an old towel nearby to wipe fingers and chisel.

Some sizing tips: Duplicate turnings can be made faster by laying out their profile on a strip of masking tape along the tool rest, with parting-tool cuts indicated by double lines. Diameters for each cut can be noted right on the tape.

If you make duplicate turnings having a tenon on one or both ends and you have trouble keeping tenon size uniform, make a simple sizer. Choose a hard block of maple or hornbeam and turn a ½-in. shank on one end to hold in the lathe's chuck. Turning this block by its shank, bore a hole in the end that's a little larger than the desired tenon size, and a little deeper than the tenon is long. If you don't have a drill bit the correct size, you can grind a drill bit slightly off-center—then it will bore a slightly larger hole. Make a ¹⁄₃₂-in. by ¹⁄₃₂-in. counterbore at the front end of the bore to help start the tenon into the hole. Remove from the lathe and remove wood off one side until you break into the bore with a gap about ¼ in. wide. Using a piece of old scraper blade, plane iron or whatever, make a flat knife as shown in the sketch at the lower left and attach it to the sizer with its cutting edge just behind the center of the gap. If you rough out your tenons to within ¹⁄₃₂ in. of size, this tool will align and finish the job accurately. Mount the sizer in the lathe chuck, and set the lathe to about 500 RPM. Hold the work in your left hand, and advance it with the tailstock crank.

If you occasionally need a few dowels of an odd size that can be made by turning down a larger dowel, you can make a fixture to do just that. If you are starting with, say, a ½-in. dowel, bore an oversized ½-in. hole through the center of a 1-in. by 3-in. by 12-in. hardwood block. Next, to support a gouge, glue and screw a smaller strip of hardwood onto the first one, with its upper edge along the centerline of the ½-in. hole. Lay a ⅜-in. or ½-in. gouge on top of this second strip, with its cutting edge overhanging the edge of the hole. Fashion a wood clamp as shown in the sketch, below right, to hold the gouge in place. Mount a ½-in. dowel in your lathe chuck, and insert the free end in the fixture hole. Run the lathe at slow speed and gently push the fixture along until it reaches the headstock. You don't need the tailstock, just support the free end of the dowel with your hand to keep it from whipping around. You'll have to fiddle a bit to find the gouge setting that produces the dowel diameter you want.

Finishing: For a high gloss, the old shellac finish is still ex-

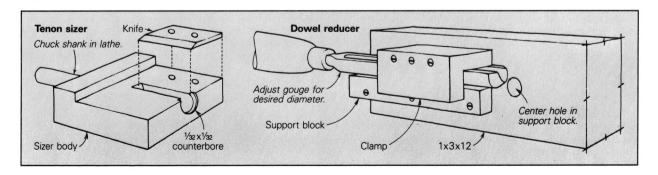

Tenon sizer — Knife — Chuck shank in lathe. — Sizer body — ¹⁄₃₂ x ¹⁄₃₂ counterbore — Dowel reducer — Adjust gouge for desired diameter. — Support block — Clamp — 1x3x12 — Center hole in support block.

cellent. With the work turning on the lathe, brush on thinned shellac until the brush starts to drag. Let the piece spin a while and repeat, being careful not to let the finish build up too much. When the surface is evenly coated and not absorbing any more shellac, let it spin a few minutes to set up. Then remove the work from the lathe and give it at least five hours to dry—overnight is best—before you smooth it with fine steel wool. Then apply paste wax, letting it dry thoroughly, and polish it on the lathe with a soft cloth.

You can obtain a fairly good instant finish by applying shellac or oil with the lathe running at high speed, and rubbing hard enough to generate heat for drying the finish. At first the surface will look glossy hard. But this method will not dry the finish that has penetrated the surface, and the interaction between the dry outer layer and the damp inner layer will eventually leave a matte finish.

Dust: Most mills have elaborate dust-removal systems. Do your lungs a favor by hanging the suction hose of your shop-vac on the lathe bed while sanding. The noise may be annoying, but it could keep you around for a few more years. □

A shop-built lathe duplicator

by Lawrence Churchill

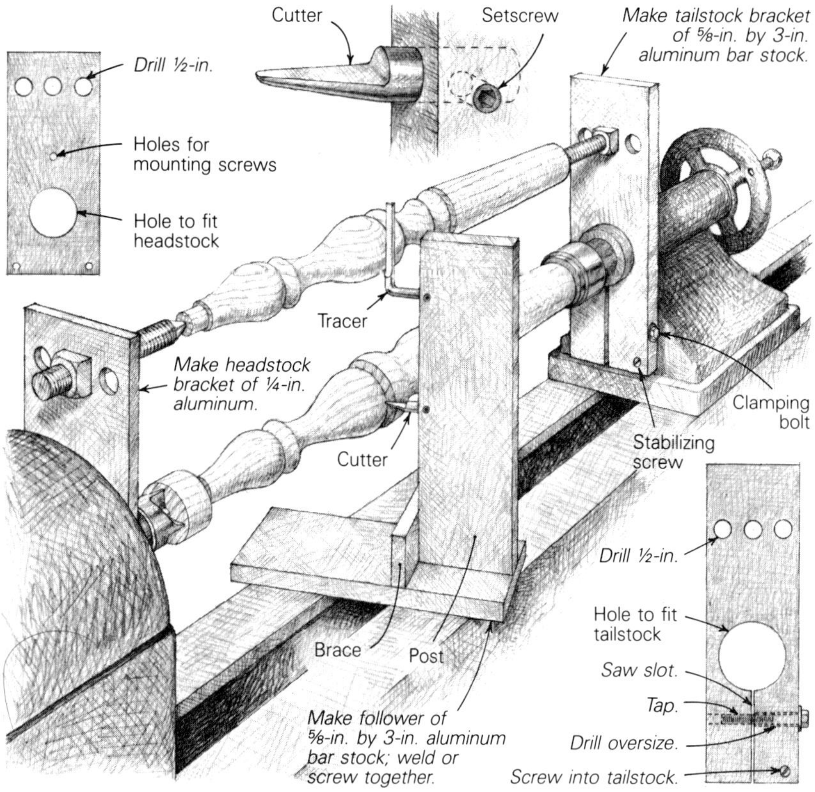

Cutter
Setscrew
Make tailstock bracket of ⅝-in. by 3-in. aluminum bar stock.
Drill ½-in.
Holes for mounting screws
Hole to fit headstock
Tracer
Make headstock bracket of ¼-in. aluminum.
Cutter
Clamping bolt
Stabilizing screw
Brace
Post
Drill ½-in.
Hole to fit tailstock
Saw slot.
Tap.
Make follower of ⅝-in. by 3-in. aluminum bar stock; weld or screw together.
Drill oversize.
Screw into tailstock.

A considerable amount of my repair work requires replacing broken chair spindles and other such matching turned parts, so a duplicator is a valuable tool. In designing the one shown here, I wanted a jig that wouldn't interfere with normal lathe operation or require any elaborate setup. My duplicator isn't robust enough to trace a part from a square blank, but once the blank has been roughed to within ¼ in. of final size, this rig will finish the job nicely.

The duplicator consists of a pair of plates attached to the lathe's headstock and tailstock, and a follower that slides along the ways. The plates allow me to mount directly over the blank either a flat pattern or, by means of a pair of auxiliary spindles in the plates, the turning I want to duplicate. The follower is

a post carrying a tracer that bears on the pattern or original turning. A cutter is mounted directly below the tracer.

First I replaced the headstock's original bearing cover plate with a piece of ¼-in. thick aluminum. This plate will hold the pattern about 4 in. above the turning axis. On some lathes you can use longer screws to attach the bracket over the original bearing cover. I made a similar bracket out of ⅝-in. by 3-in. aluminum bar to fit over the tailstock spindle housing. Aluminum bar can be jigsawn or bandsawn with ordinary woodcutting blades.

Drill the three ½-in. holes in the headstock plate as shown, then slide the tailstock and its plate up to it and use dowel centers to transfer the holes. To hold the part you want to duplicate,

mount a pointed length of ½-in. threaded rod in the center hole of each plate, with a nut on both sides. A flat pattern can be copied by cutting two tenons on each end and wedging these in the plates' outer holes.

The follower consists of two lengths of ⅝-in. by 3-in. aluminum bar, joined at right angles and rigidly braced. These parts could be heliarc-welded, but I just screw them together. At the lathe-center height, drill a ¼-in. hole for the cutting tool, then cross-drill and tap for a setscrew. Do the same about 1 in. below the pattern centerline, for the tracer. A broken ¼-in. diameter tap or an old drill ground to a pencil-shaped cone and then ground flat on top makes a scraping-type cutter. Make the tracer by bending a 4-in. length of steel rod to a right angle and grinding its vertical profile to the shape of the cutter. Mount and adjust these parts so that when the edge of the tracer touches the pattern, the cutter cuts that diameter.

Most old turnings to be copied are out-of-round (egg-shaped) and bowed. If you position the original with the bow up or down, it won't affect the reproduction; that's why the tracer is so long. The variation in egg-shaped parts is usually not significant, except on tenons, which should be gauged for a close fit.

Start with the regular tool rest and rough out the new part in the normal manner. Most turners can get pretty close by eye, and having the pattern near the work makes it even easier—you can sight directly down from the pattern to check your work. When the new part is roughed out, remove the standard tool rest and move its base off to one side. Then just guide the follower to trim the new turning to final size. Polish and wax the follower base to keep it sliding smoothly. In my shop, this simple system has turned those duplicating jobs from red ink to black. □

Lawrence Churchill works wood in Mayville, Wis.

Lathe speeds

by R. Perry Mercurio

What is the right speed for a lathe, and what can you do about it? Assuming you have the usual set of carbon-steel tools, speeds for spindle turning should range between 750 RPM and 2500 RPM. Ultimately, we are concerned with the speed at which the surface of the work is turning, not merely the speed of the lathe. Thus, the larger the diameter of the work, the slower the lathe should turn.

But surface speed isn't the only consideration. Let's say you have a stair baluster about 1½ in. in diameter and 30 in. long. Even though the diameter is small, you can see right away that the length should limit the speed, unless you want to risk getting a faceful of wood—a speed of 800 RPM will be fast enough. If you have a workpiece only about 10 in. long and perhaps 2 in. in diameter, you can go to top speed, unless the species of wood comes into play. Harder woods create more friction, quickly heating the tool, which will then require more sharpening. Go slower. Some woods, teak for example, contain abrasive minerals, and require slower speed as well as more frequent sharpening.

Add a countershaft: If your lathe has only the usual three or four speed possibilities and you are beginning to get serious about turning, you will want to add more speed changes. An easy way is to put a countershaft between the motor and lathe headstock, with a step pulley at each end, as shown in the drawing below. Belt one end of the shaft to the motor and the other end to the headstock pulley. The countershaft frame should be hinged and should also have a locking device. This will ease belt changes and cut down vibration. The motor mount should be attached in the same manner. With this setup you can change speeds easily and quickly.

A word of caution: it's surprisingly easy when switching belts around to end up with the opposite of what you thought you were doing. A large bowl blank revving up to 2500 RPM can give you quite a start. So figure out the speeds at various belt positions and make a chart to hang on the wall behind the lathe. The formula is simple: merely multiply the driver speed by the diameter of its pulley and divide the product by the diameter of the driven pulley. With V-belts and pulleys this method is approximate, but close enough.

Bowlturning can get you into a really low range of speeds, especially for larger bowls. You might want to choose a set of pulleys that get down to 200 RPM, or even less. A lot will also depend upon the rigidity of your lathe and how well it is anchored to the floor.

Reverse: It's a real help to be able to reverse the spindle rotation. Perhaps the most common benefit is being able to sand off laid-down fibers. But suppose you are making a dozen small bowls or bases that are being turned on a screw center. During the process of turning, sanding and finishing, you will have to mount and unmount each one several times. How easy it is to hit your switch either right or left to screw them on or off the headstock. When turning the interior of a bowl or dish, reverse allows you to work on the far side of the center, giving you improved vision and tool handling. Take care, however, that your work is securely fastened and that the faceplate is tight, else it might unscrew in the event of a dig.

Most motors can be reversed by swapping two wires in the junction box. Obtain a drum-type reversing switch from an electrical supplier and mount it over the lathe headstock. Connect it so that when the handle is pushed to the right, rotation is normal. Do not mount the switch where you could accidentally turn it on. Some professional turners like an on/off foot switch on the floor. This allows them to start or stop the lathe to inspect the work without losing hand position on the chisel. A foot switch and a drum-reversing switch can be wired so they work together. □

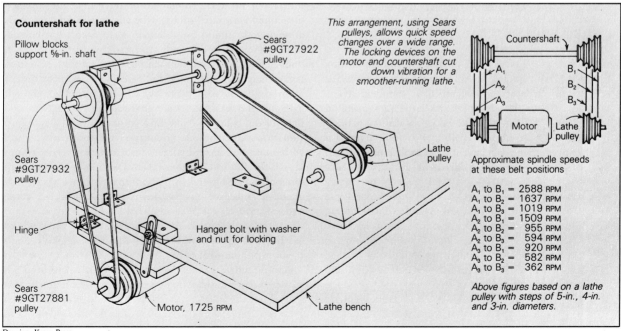

Countershaft for lathe

Pillow blocks support ⅝-in. shaft

Sears #9GT27922 pulley

Sears #9GT27932 pulley

Hinge

Sears #9GT27881 pulley

Hanger bolt with washer and nut for locking

Motor, 1725 RPM

Lathe bench

Lathe pulley

This arrangement, using Sears pulleys, allows quick speed changes over a wide range. The locking devices on the motor and countershaft cut down vibration for a smoother-running lathe.

Countershaft

Motor   Lathe pulley

Approximate spindle speeds at these belt positions

A_1 to B_1 = 2588 RPM
A_1 to B_2 = 1637 RPM
A_1 to B_3 = 1019 RPM
A_2 to B_1 = 1509 RPM
A_2 to B_2 = 955 RPM
A_2 to B_3 = 594 RPM
A_3 to B_1 = 920 RPM
A_3 to B_2 = 582 RPM
A_3 to B_3 = 362 RPM

Above figures based on a lathe pulley with steps of 5-in., 4-in. and 3-in. diameters.

Drawing: Karen Pease

How to Make a Wooden Flute

Lathe-boring long holes, and keeping them centered

by Whittaker Freegard

Fig. 1: Measurements for a six-hole flute

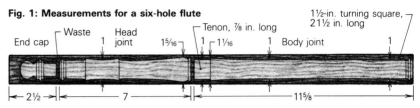

Cut the flute blank with minimal waste between sections to ensure matching grain. Dimensions are important if the flute is to play in tune.

My first attempt at making a flute was a turned piece of pine, bored with a brace and bit. It didn't work. The next time, I drilled the tube with spade bits in a Jacobs chuck in the lathe. The flute could be played, but my processes were slow and uncertain, and the results sometimes unpredictable.

Over the years, I've improved my techniques, and learned enough about the precise anatomy of flutes to make one with precision and within a reasonable amount of time. Basically, a blank is rough-turned round, the inner diameter is bored, then the blank is mounted on a wooden mandrel for turning the tube to its final diameter. This ensures that the bore is exactly centered, one of the most important details in flute making. Length, finger-hole location and wall thickness all must be in balance for a successful instrument. I rely heavily on lathe accessories to make my flutes, but you don't actually need all the equipment I have to make a single flute; I've outlined some alternatives on p. 22. If you would like to increase the versatility of your lathe for such projects as tall lamps, drilled-out containers, and even a little metalworking, however, the bits and chucks I talk about here are a worthwhile investment. Mine paid for themselves a long time ago.

Preparing the blank—The flute shown here has a detachable head joint and is tuned to a G-major scale. If you want another pitch or a different sound qual-

Whittaker Freegard has made flutes under the shop name of Garett Alden for over ten years in Mendocino County, Cal., and Eureka Springs, Ark.

ity, you can experiment with other dimensions. Generally, large or long bores produce lower tones; narrower and shorter bores, higher ones. Thick walls give a richer but less responsive sound; thin walls, a thinner, breathier tone.

The denser and more resinous a wood, the fuller and richer the tone. My consistent favorite is cocobolo, although many exotic and domestic hardwoods produce excellent tones. In general, select a wood with as closed grain as possible, but avoid rock maple. It is exasperatingly hard on shell augers, and unless sealed with epoxy, it has a dry, thin tone. My favorite native hardwoods are black walnut and cherry, especially when the wood is burled or compressed. I buy 6/4 or 8/4 lumber and bandsaw the planks into 1½-in. turning squares. To allow for the jointed flute's body tenon, and the end cap for the head joint, I cut each blank to 21½ in., making sure that the blank is free of checks.

Measuring as shown in figure 1, I cut the body, head joint and end cap to length, and mark the top and bottom ends of each piece. The figure pattern will appear different when the square is rounded, and it's all too easy to end up with mismatched sections.

I use a spur center in the headstock to mount the head joint and body section

in the lathe. To reduce vibration, I round each blank with a large gouge, then I use a wide cut-off tool to make a 1-in. long tenon on the tailstock end, so it will slide snugly into my shopmade ball-bearing hollow tailstock, shown in figure 3. The drill bits pass through the center of this hollow tailstock to bore out the instrument. Then I cut a ½-in. long step in the headstock end to fit a 3-jaw chuck. I cut this step larger than the final flute diameter, because the full length of the blank is needed.

Boring out—At this point, the lathe changes from a turning tool to a boring tool. As shown in figure 3, lathes can bore from either end. Boring each section of a flute to final diameter is best done in three steps, beginning with a short pilot hole. In the second step, a hand-held bit extends the pilot through the blank, and the third step expands the center hole to its full diameter. To begin the pilot hole, as shown in figure 3A, I hold the work in a 3-jaw chuck and support the tailstock end in the ball-bearing hollow tailstock. I mount a ½-in. twist bit in a Jacobs chuck in the tailstock. The hollow tailstock must be adjusted so that the bit lines up exactly with the center of the blank. With the work turning at the lathe's slowest

From *Fine Woodworking* magazine (January 1984) 44:64-67

Fig. 2: Parts of a flute

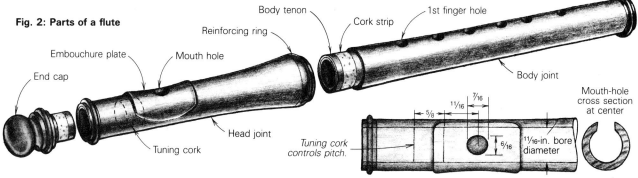

Body tenon
1st finger hole
Reinforcing ring
Cork strip
Embouchure plate
Mouth hole
End cap
Tuning cork
Head joint
Body joint
Tuning cork controls pitch.

Mouth-hole cross section at center

5/8 11/16 7/16 6/16 11/16-in. bore diameter

Fig. 3: Three setups for boring on the lathe

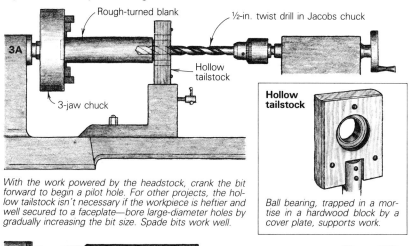

3A
Rough-turned blank
½-in. twist drill in Jacobs chuck
3-jaw chuck
Hollow tailstock

Hollow tailstock

With the work powered by the headstock, crank the bit forward to begin a pilot hole. For other projects, the hollow tailstock isn't necessary if the workpiece is heftier and well secured to a faceplate—bore large-diameter holes by gradually increasing the bit size. Spade bits work well.

Ball bearing, trapped in a mortise in a hardwood block by a cover plate, supports work.

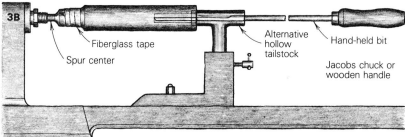

3B
Fiberglass tape
Spur center
Alternative hollow tailstock
Hand-held bit
Jacobs chuck or wooden handle

*Bore a full-length pilot hole with a hand-held shell auger. The author uses the chuck and tailstock shown in step **A**, but the setup shown in **B** will work too (see box, p. 66). As explained in the main text, full diameter is next bored with a hand-held Planetor bit, following the pilot hole.*

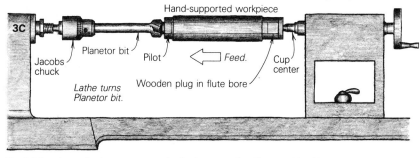

Hand-supported workpiece
3C
Jacobs chuck
Planetor bit
Pilot
Feed.
Cup center
Wooden plug in flute bore
Lathe turns Planetor bit.

To slightly enlarge the bore to accept the body tenon, fit a Planetor bit with a pilot that matches the bore diameter, then crank the work forward into the bit's cutting spurs. A piloted spade bit will also enlarge holes, but may split thin-walled turnings.

Bored and turned on the lathe, this 19-in. rosewood flute (left) has ends and center joint reinforced by rings of water buffalo horn. To make a flute, a ½-in. dia. pilot hole is first bored with the 30-in. long shell auger (bottom), which cuts into end grain without wandering. The Planetor bit (center) follows the pilot hole by means of a shopmade center insert, a wooden or metal plug turned to fit the pilot hole. The coiled spring ejects chips. Both bits are hand-held and fed into the work as it turns.

speed, about 750 RPM, I crank the tailstock forward to drill a 2-in. deep hole. The rigidity of the tailstock ensures that the hole starts straight. Then I remove the tailstock from the lathe bed.

To bore the full length, I use two specialized bits, shown in the photo at the bottom of these pages. Unless the wood grain is particularly uneven, a shell auger will bore a long, straight hole without wandering. Once started into the pilot hole, it cuts on-center, aligning itself with the stationary centerpoint of the turning work. As shown in figure 3B, the bit is held freehand, not in the tailstock chuck, and is pushed into the work in short steps. Feeding the bit into the wood by hand is a great pleasure, and not nearly as difficult as it may sound. Withdraw the bit from time to time to clear the chips, and be careful that you don't get the bit so hot that its cutting edge loses its temper. This full-length hole is the pilot for the final bore.

To bore to full diameter, I use an 11/16-in. Planetor bit, which has an 18-in. shank and a coiled chip ejector. My model is an older one, but you can still get the equivalent from the source listed at the end of this article. The Planetor bit is also hand-held, but for a better grip I tighten it into a Jacobs chuck. This completes the boring in the body joint, but the head joint still requires a socket to accept the tenon on the body.

To make the socket, I bore from the headstock end, as shown in figure 3C. I remove the 3-jaw chuck and install a ½-in. Jacobs chuck, fitted with a short 1-in. Planetor bit with an 11/16-in. pilot center. I remove the hollow tailstock and remount the regular tailstock, fitted with a cup center. To center the flute blank on the tailstock, I push a hardwood plug into the end of the bore. The tailstock should be adjusted so that the blank is supported by the Planetor bit's pilot, but not pressed against the cutting spurs. With the lathe at its slowest speed, I support the blank with my left hand and slowly turn the tailstock crank to push the blank ⅞ in. into the bit. This completes the head-joint boring.

Turning the outside on a mandrel— To turn the outside of the flute, I support the blank on a mandrel, a rod that extends through the blank and projects an inch or more at each end. I make mandrels from birch dowels, turning them down until they make a snug sliding fit in the bore. Better a little loose than too tight, so occasionally I use some thin paper or wooden shims between the mandrel and the blank, taking care that the mandrel is centered in the bore.

To help protect the ends of the flute from splitting, you may want to add reinforcing rings, which also provide a visual transition between the sections. I used water buffalo horn on the flute shown here, but rings can also be made from brass tubing, soldered silver sheet, or cow horn. To make them from brass tubing, mount the tube on a mandrel on the lathe, and with a jewelers' saw, saw off as many rings as you need. Rings should be put onto the blanks before the outside profile is turned. Cut a seat into the blank to fit the inner diameter of the ring, apply some glue, and

tap the ring into place. Horn rings are fitted oversize, then turned down at the same time as the blank.

Turn the tenon on the body so that it makes a good sliding fit in the head-joint socket. To ensure an airtight seal, I glue a ½-in. wide strip of cork in a shallow groove around the tenon. Bevel one end of the cork strip so that the joint overlaps, apply yellow glue, and clamp with a rubber band. When the glue is dry, carefully sand the strip down while the body is turning. When checking the fit, apply a little cork grease (available from any music store) for lubrication. Otherwise, the fit will end up too loose.

Next I turn the outside profile of the flute. Pay careful attention to the diameters in figure 1, because they determine final wall thickness. If you'd like a raised mouthpiece, called an embouchure plate, which some people feel makes a flute easier to play, turn the area oversize and carve away the unwanted wood by hand before sanding. Sand and polish the flute with progressively finer grades of paper, finishing with a worn 600-grit. Final polishing is done with the grain, with the motor off. After I have polished the flute sections, I make the end cap, a short section that slides snugly into the top end of the

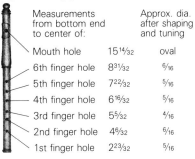

Fig 4: Drilling guide

Measurements from bottom end to center of:		Approx. dia. after shaping and tuning
Mouth hole	15¹⁴⁄₃₂	oval
6th finger hole	8³¹⁄₃₂	6/16
5th finger hole	7²²⁄₃₂	5/16
4th finger hole	6¹⁶⁄₃₂	5/16
3rd finger hole	5⁵⁄₃₂	4/16
2nd finger hole	4⁶⁄₃₂	6/16
1st finger hole	2²³⁄₃₂	5/16

head joint. It, too, has a cork inlay, and can be topped off by turning a short ornamental end. All of the sections can now be put together. Remember to use a liberal amount of cork grease, and don't force the fit, or the socket may split. If the socket is too tight, carefully sand or file the cork.

The holes— Measuring as shown in figure 4, and keeping the mouth hole and finger holes in a straight line, mark and indent the center of each hole. To prevent tearout, insert a softwood dowel in the bore before you drill. To drill the mouth hole, support the head joint in a V-block or a handscrew on the drill-press table, and use a ⅜-in. brad-point bit. To ensure that the hole will be in the right place, align the point of the bit with the mark on the blank, and clamp things down before you drill. Change to a ¼-in. bit and drill the finger holes.

I undercut and shape the mouth hole with round files and narrow knife blades. Figure 2 on p. 21 shows a typical cross-section at the center of the hole. I prefer an oval mouth hole, but its shape has been a subject of debate throughout the flute's history. Most mouth holes are undercut on the edge against which your airstream is directed, although the amount of undercutting is again a matter of preference. I feel that too little angle rather than too much is better, to achieve maximum control and flexibility in playing. The finger holes, too, will require undercutting and enlarging for the flute to play in tune.

After the holes are drilled, sand the bore. I slit a dowel, slip the edge of a sandpaper strip into it and wrap the paper around the dowel. You can use the sanding rod manually or chucked in the lathe headstock, using progressively finer grits to produce a smooth bore.

Next make the tuning cork, which blocks the tube just above the mouth hole and controls the pitch. First, run a

Some low-tech boring setups

The simplest hollow tailstock consists of a copper-pipe T-fitting, as shown in figure 3B on p. 21, supported by the tool-rest base. To make the blank fit it, bore a shallow seating hole, the outer diameter of the pipe, in the end of the blank, using a spade bit. An electric drill will be accurate enough. Lubricate the seat with spray silicone once in a while as it turns. Silicone will penetrate the wood and interfere with any finish you apply, so to prevent problems, cut off the end of the blank after boring. Chances are that the first couple of inches of the bore will be enlarged because of the number of times you have to remove and reinsert the bit, so you should plan some extra length to be cut off anyway.

The copper won't be stiff enough to hold the blank firmly against a spur center in the headstock, but if you rough-turn the end round and tape it to the headstock with fiberglass tape, the setup will work without a 3-jaw chuck.

Extra-long twist bits (bellhangers' bits) are no substitute for a shell auger.

Twist bits wander when boring end grain, and you will scrap a lot of blanks before you get a straight hole. Twist drills can enlarge a pilot hole, however, working up bit by bit until the bore is full-size. A series of larger and larger spade bits with extensions could also be used. Extend a spade bit for light-duty boring by lapping and silver-soldering it to ¼-in. steel rod stock. This modified spade bit has the advantage of being able to bore a long hole without clogging on its own chips, which twist bits invariably do. Clamp vise-grips to the end of the rod as a handle, and mark any long bit so that you don't bore too far. There's nothing quite like the sound of a shell auger jamming into the spur center—expensive "music."

Another way, adequate for shorter holes, calls for spade bits in a Jacobs chuck in the headstock. Leave the blank square. Clamp blocks to the tool rest to form a support track that will let you move the work into the bit by advancing the tailstock. —W.F.

Playing the flute

Some people produce a sound the first time they try, others may have to practice for days. Blowing across, not into, the mouth hole (as in blowing across a bottle top) causes the stream of air to be split by the opposite edge of the hole, creating the tone. By slightly rolling the mouth hole toward or away from your lips, you can hear the tone become clearer, then fade. Aim the airstream carefully, and use the least amount of air that will produce a strong, clear tone.

When you can confidently produce a tone, try playing a scale. Be sure the pads of your fingers completely cover the finger holes. The fingering chart shows a major scale as Do, Re, Mi, with sharps and flats between. Another way to play sharps and flats is by covering only half of the finger hole. The second octave is fingered the same, but with more air pressure. You can add color and variety by rolling or sliding your fingers off a hole, a more advanced technique that allows you to subtly change the pitch of any note. —*W.F.*

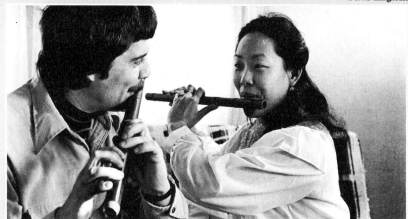

Freegard and wife, Nanita, show correct hand and mouth positions for flute-playing.

Fig. 5: Fingering chart, chromatic scale

		Do		Re		Mi	Fa		Sol		La		Ti	Do
Left hand	1st finger	●	●	●	●	●	●	●	●	●	●	○	○	○
	2nd finger	●	●	●	●	●	●	●	●	○	○	●	○	●
	3rd finger	●	●	●	●	●	●	○	○	●	○	○	○	●
Right hand	1st finger	●	●	●	●	●	○	●	○	○	○	○	○	●
	2nd finger	●	●	●	○	○	○	○	○	●	○	○	○	●
	3rd finger	●	◐	○	●	○	○	○	○	●	○	○	○	●

pencil point around the top inside edge of the bore, and then press the head joint against the end of a ⅝-in. long piece of bottle cork. The graphite will leave a mark of the bore's diameter. With a knife, shave the cork around the pencil line, test it for fit, then push it into place, ¹¹⁄₁₆ in. from the center of the mouth hole. Once the cork is in place, you should be able to get a clean, flute-like tone by blowing across the mouth hole. The tone will be much improved when you oil the flute—use a light, non-toxic oil (such as mineral oil or safflower oil), and be sure to wipe off all the excess, so that there is no oil buildup.

The tuning process may sound mysterious and complicated, but it is neither if done methodically. We have deliberately drilled undersized holes, because it's best to tune each note by enlarging the hole, rather than by constricting it by adding substances such as beeswax.

It may take some practice to produce a clear, reliable tone, necessary for tuning your instrument. Refer to the playing instructions in the box above, and if you are still uncertain, enlist the aid of a flute-playing friend. If you can't hear when the flute is in tune, try playing the scale along with a well-tuned piano, another instrument or an electronic tuner.

With all of the sections together, the tonic note (all six finger holes covered), G in this case, should be in tune, while the finger holes will sound flat in various degrees. If the tonic note itself is flat, you can sharpen it by flaring the end of the tube up to the first finger hole. If the note is sharp, pull out the tenon a little. Start the finger-hole tuning at the bottom hole (A) and slowly work your way up the scale, playing back and forth to recheck previous tuning. In the first octave, enlarge the diameter of each hole to sharpen the pitch. Undercutting the inside edge of a hole will also sharpen the pitch, and help the response of a sluggish note, but this is best saved for tuning the second octave. As a tuning overview, leave the third hole from the bottom (C) small. The two holes you will have to enlarge the most are the second finger holes on both hands—B on the right hand, E on the left.

Tuning the two octaves together is called the fine-tuning, and is done completely with undercutting after the first octave is in tune. Undercutting the upper edge of a hole raises the pitch for the first and second octaves; undercutting the lower edge raises the pitch in the second octave, and has only a very slight effect in the first octave. This is especially helpful since the second octave tends to be flatter in general than the first. If you remove too much wood, add a little beeswax. Heat the tip of a nail, melt a drop of wax with it, and transfer the wax to the rim of the hole.

Lightly oil the wood once or twice a year so it doesn't dry out, and try to keep the flute from extremes of temperature and humidity. After playing, gently swab the moisture from the bore. If you leave the flute assembled for too long a period, the tenon cork may become compressed, loosening the fit. A remedy is to dampen the cork and heat it briefly with a match, but be careful not to scorch it. □

Sources (1984 prices) _____
Shell augers: Woodcraft Supply, 41 Atlantic Ave., PO Box 4000, Woburn, Mass. 01888. About $30.

Planetor bits: Rule Industries, Cape Ann Industrial Park, Gloucester, Mass. 01930, (617) 281-0440. Catalog PB-83.

Bore—P-69L (12-in. shaft with chip ejector), ¹¹⁄₁₆-in. dia., $22.50; 5½-in. shank extension XJ-55, $5.75.

Socket—P-100 (1-in. dia. bit), $12.75; 3½-in. shank SB-35, $5.35.

Sheet cork: International Violin Company, Ltd., 4026 West Belvedere Ave., Baltimore, Md. 21215.

Water buffalo horn: Don Kostecki, 6245 N. Fairfield, Chicago, Ill. 60659.

Slender turnings—*I do custom woodturning, and while I have no problem with bulky parts like Victorian newel posts or balusters, slender chair spindles and other small parts give me fits. Turning them between centers in the usual way provides too little support, and the parts tend to vibrate and break under the force of a cutting tool. I realize that many of the parts I'm asked to duplicate were produced on automatic lathes; nevertheless, there must be some freehand techniques for controlling small-diameter work.*
—*Paul Mahany, Bethesda, Md.*

RICHARD STARR REPLIES: Slender turnings flex in two ways—they bend and they twist. Bending occurs when you push the tool against the wood, and rather than surrendering the shaving, the wood resists and tries to climb the tool's edge. At best, you get a chattering, intermittent cut. At worst, you break the piece. Twist occurs as you work a thin turning some distance from the driven end. The wood resists the tool and winds up like a spring, which then releases and overcomes the tool. The result is spiral-shaped chatter marks.

To keep the wood from bending, some turners use a steady rest, which clamps to the lathe ways and supports the wood near where the tool is cutting. The drawing shows one

Wedge weighted with lead pivots rest against work

Notch supports work

Pivot

design for a steady, taken from F. Pain's *The Practical Wood Turner* (Sterling, 2 Park Ave., N.Y., N.Y. 10016), an excellent reference book on turning.

I prefer to use my hand to steady the work. I hold the tool with my right hand, so I place my left thumb on the top surface of the tool, curling my fingers around the work and supporting it against bending as I cut. Friction heats the hand, which is why old-timers pause often to cool the palm on the lathe's pulley housing. Keep your tool sharp and take fine cuts to keep cutting resistance—and twisting—low. For cylindrical and tapered turnings, limit twisting by using a hand plane instead of a turning tool. You can control the plane's depth of cut and there's no danger of digging in. Try a block plane with a sharp iron set for a fine cut. Steady the tool as shown in the photo, with the edge of the blade swung at least 45° to the axis of the work. Travel slowly along the work in the direction the plane is pointing.

On very long pieces, you can reduce twisting by reversing and rechucking, so you are always working the half nearest the headstock. If you have a 3- or 4-jaw chuck that's hollow in the center, you can just project the work through it, extending the turning and moving the tailstock as you go. Keep the lathe speed low, because a thin, flexible piece could whip off the lathe if run too fast.

Old-fashioned turners' gauges you can make yourself

by John Rodd

Before machines did the job, production turners used a number of devices that have since become rare. Yet their use may be of more than passing interest to turners today. Old-fashioned tools are often ingenious solutions to special problems, and most of them can easily be made. The sizing tool for instance, labeled *A* on the next page, was made when carpenters used spoon and center bits. These were of irregular size because sharpening would reduce the cutting diameter. For that reason Old Charlie (a woodturner friend), on receiving an order for a set of banisters, would ask for a sample hole. Once he had fitted a pin to the hole he had only to set the gap in the sizing tool to it, turn each pin slightly oversize (and he could do that quite closely by eye) and bring down the tool, which would cut a groove of the required fit. It was then a matter of seconds to finish the rest of the pin. If you should be turning a piece to a given size, you need not attempt the hand-forging and artistic attention to detail that went into the specimen pictured. You can make one out of brass, as shown in the drawing, to fit an existing parting tool.

But odd-sized pins are rare nowadays, and the set-gauge *(B)* has probably done more work for me than all the other gauges combined. I see by my center-punch work that I made it in 1940. At that time I had gotten to know the chief saw-filer at one of the local mills and was able to get from him scraps of the head band saw, which was ⅛ in. thick by about

12 in. wide. With an abrasive cutting wheel I ground out slots in this material, covering a range from ¼ in. to ⅝ in. by sixteenths and on to 1 in. by eighths. It is a hard steel, in no danger of bending, so I can press it on to an oversized pin and move left and right to produce a tight fit. Usually I undercut the shoulder with a skew chisel used as a scraper to make sure the edge will come up flush.

Tool *C* is a similar sizing tool, made around the turn of the century by P. H. Neild with a span of from ¾ in. to 1½ in. The steps are long enough to reach the diameter but not to feel the fit, and so I have used it only a little.

Tool *D* is a disc caliper by the same maker. It consists of two *L*-shaped, slotted steel plates, held together by two bolts and wing nuts. Below the head of each bolt is an elongated key that fits the slot in the plates and prevents the bolt from turning when the nut is tightened.

An explanation of the steps required to produce a gross of breadboards led me to make the radius gauge *(E)*. At that time a Mr. Willows had a used-furniture business but he had started life as a faceplate turner, mass-producing such items as small dished tabletops, alms dishes, breadboards and *paterae*. Never, he told me, had he turned anything between centers. I asked him about making breadboards.

With few exceptions, an old breadboard will show no mark of where a screw or nails held it while being turned. Instead,

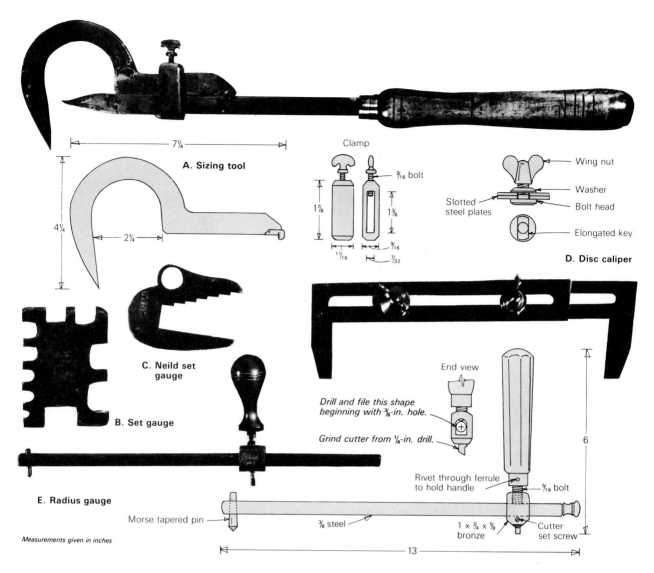

A. Sizing tool

Clamp

$\frac{3}{16}$ bolt

$7\frac{1}{4}$

$4\frac{1}{4}$

$2\frac{1}{4}$

$1\frac{7}{8}$

$1\frac{3}{8}$

$\frac{9}{16}$

$\frac{11}{16}$

$\frac{7}{32}$

Wing nut

Washer

Bolt head

Slotted steel plates

Elongated key

D. Disc caliper

C. Neild set gauge

B. Set gauge

End view

Drill and file this shape beginning with $\frac{3}{8}$-in. hole.

Grind cutter from $\frac{1}{4}$-in. drill.

Rivet through ferrule to hold handle

$\frac{5}{16}$ bolt

6

E. Radius gauge

Morse tapered pin

$\frac{3}{8}$ steel

$1 \times \frac{3}{4} \times \frac{5}{8}$ bronze

Cutter set screw

Measurements given in inches

13

the design of the bottom will include a ring, projecting about $\frac{1}{8}$ in. from the general surface, which the chuck gripped while the top was being turned. The process was as follows: A disc about the same size as the board was mounted on the lathe, faced off and then furnished with a ring of brads about $\frac{1}{4}$ in. in from the edge; the brads were clipped to a length of $\frac{3}{16}$ in., then filed sharp. The blank to be turned would be impaled on them and quite adequately held while the bottom was turned and sanded to include a raised ring. The whole batch, usually a gross, would receive this treatment.

To turn the face, a second disc would now be mounted and a recess turned in it providing a tight fit on the bottom rings. The fit required a mallet and block to mount the first two or three boards; later, a few blows with the heel of the hand would suffice. It requires skill and judgment, especially in the first cuts near the perimeter, to avoid dislodging the board, but Mr. Willows assured me that a gross would normally be finished in a single chuck. He would remove the ring of holes caused by the brad points when shaping the edge.

The uniformity of the diameter of the bottom rings was of course essential and explains the need for the radius gauge. It consists of a cutter, whose distance from the conical pin at the other end of a trammel bar is adjustable to the required radius by means of a set-screw-cum-handle, which is attached directly above the cutter. After having faced up, you center

the blank with the point of a skew chisel and hold the conical pin against the center. Press the cutter into the work to form the ring.

When making my radius gauge, as with most workshop tools and jigs, the design was influenced by the availability of materials, which is why the drawing differs from the actual tool, *E*. The bar is a piece of $\frac{3}{8}$-in. cold-rolled steel, 13 in. long; the fancy filing to the right is just decoration. The pin to the left is a Morse taper pin with the thick end filed to a conical point while revolving in an electric drill. I drilled and reamed a suitable hole to receive it. The sliding member is a piece of bronze $\frac{5}{8}$ in. by $\frac{3}{4}$ in. by 1 in., bored lengthwise with a $\frac{1}{4}$-in. hole for the cutter and threaded for a $\frac{5}{16}$-in. S.A.E. screw at the other end for the set-screw-cum-handle. Drill and file the cross hole for the bar to fit. The handle can be bored and threaded and the set screw cemented in with epoxy and riveted through the ferrule as shown, or it can be filed to a tang and driven in. The cutter is a $\frac{1}{4}$-in. drill ground as shown and secured with a set screw. Mine was ground to a slight taper and driven into a $\frac{15}{64}$-in. hole. If you snap the drill it will be hard at the break but be careful not to soften it while reducing it to shape. □

John Rodd, author of Restoring and Repairing Antique Furniture, *lives in Sidney, B.C.*

Making Period Bedposts

Methods from the Deep South

by Asher Carmichael

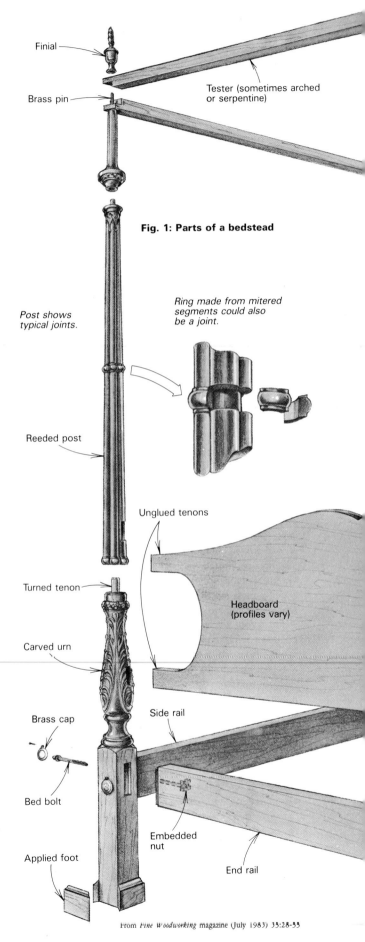

Finial

Brass pin

Tester (sometimes arched or serpentine)

Fig. 1: Parts of a bedstead

Post shows typical joints.

Ring made from mitered segments could also be a joint.

Reeded post

Unglued tenons

Turned tenon

Headboard (profiles vary)

Carved urn

Brass cap

Side rail

Bed bolt

Embedded nut

Applied foot

End rail

A spinning beam 4 in. square and up to 7 ft. long has a lot of inertia, and turning one into a bedpost might seem a frightful task. Yet in the course of visiting several bed makers in the Mobile area, I discovered that proper planning and some ingenious jigs can take the risk and the mystery out of the job. Mobile is a bedmaking center, the home of one major bed manufacturer, Reid Classics, and a few one-man shops as well. The jigs and fixtures shown in this article can be used not only for bedposts, but for any long turnings.

The Reid Classics story began some 50 years ago, when Robert Reid went to work for Roy Blake, a cabinetmaker who specialized in restoring and reproducing the many antiques found in the Mobile area. After WW II, Reid and his brother Julian opened a general woodworking shop that in its early years made everything from horse-drawn carriages to tennis rackets. Because of demand, they eventually specialized in period four-poster beds. Over the years, they have devised machine-production methods that still maintain the uncompromising excellence of detail they had learned from Blake (who in his late seventies still does some work in a one-room shop in his home).

The Reids have, over the years, done their best to perpetuate their methods and the traditions that Blake started. Of the three other bedmakers in the area, two—Milton Collins and Glenn De-Gruy—worked for the Reids for years before starting their own shops, and the third, William Blake, learned his craft from his uncle Roy, the same old master who steered Robert Reid into woodworking so many years before.

Beds are knockdown construction so that they can be moved. A typical four-poster is shown in the photo on the facing page. End rails and side rails—usually 2 in. thick and 5 in. wide—are tenoned to fit into mortises cut in square sections of the posts, as shown in figure 1, then held in place with long bolts and embedded nuts. The standard hardware used in the 18th century is still available today from many local hardware stores and, if not, period-hardware suppliers such as Horton Brasses (Box 120F, Cromwell, Conn. 06416) will have them.

The headboard is never glued in place. It is kept from loosening by the location of the bed bolts—the bolts securing the end rails are above the ones in the side rails, so that they constantly pull in on the posts and the headboard. The tester (pronounced teester, and often spelled that way in old records) is sometimes straight and rectangular, sometimes arched or serpentine. The top of each post carries a brass or steel pin that passes through

From *Fine Woodworking* magazine (July 1983) 33:28-33

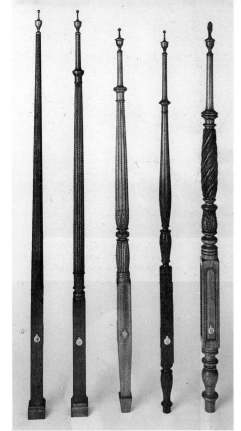

Shown chronologically left to right are posts in the Chippendale, Hepplewhite, Sheraton and early Victorian styles. A lightly draped bed with serpentine tester is shown at right.

the tester to hold it in place. The finial then slides onto the pin to conceal it. In Colonial days, testers carried the weight of voluminous side curtains of expensive imported fabric, which could completely enclose the bed and its occupants. A richly draped bed provided privacy and shelter from drafts, and showed off the family's wealth as well. One old document lists 56 yards of material ordered as bed "furniture," which is what they called the fabric. Today's four-posters are seldom so fully furnished.

Mattresses, filled with up to 40 pounds of down, were at first supported on thick stuffed pads laid directly on the floor, but methods of raising them up on webs of rope and canvas were soon devised, with the ropes secured through holes or pins in the rails. Reproduction beds are usually adapted to take standard box springs in the same ways used for regular beds.

The Reid shop makes scores of period designs by combining about thirty different posts with various headboards and testers. By studying bedposts in museums, and making templates of antique posts that come in for repair, the Reid shop has accumulated authentic patterns that span periods from early Chippendale to late Victorian. As a rough guide, Chippendale's influence shows in cabriole legs with ball-and-claw feet, and also in square posts with applied foot moldings. Hepplewhite's style had reeding instead of the earlier fluted designs and Sheraton introduced round, tapering legs. Such distinctions are not always easy to make because styles and influences overlapped. The tall posts favored up to around 1820 soon gave way to heavier designs with shorter posts, no drapery, and sometimes even fancy foot rails in addition to the structural members. Such changes marked the end of an era. As Wallace Nutting once wryly wrote: "A foot rail did not come in until good styles went out."

The furnituremaker in the 18th century often turned bedposts in one piece except for the finial. In those days, turning a one-

piece post had advantages. For one thing, their boring tools were probably not as efficient as today's, and it would have been difficult to drill accurate dowel holes to join a post made in sections. In addition, turners used manually powered lathes, which allowed them a range of slow speeds that took most of the danger out of turning long, heavy stock. This and the use of a steady rest diminished the tendency of slender work to whip and vibrate.

A few of the shops in the Mobile area have lengthened their lathes to accept longer than usual work. One approach is to remove the headstock and tailstock from a standard lathe, and then make new lathe ways from heavy angle iron. The headstock and tailstock are attached by whatever means is practical, and the whole assembly is raised up on a sturdy wooden stand. Another way to lengthen a lathe is to remove the tailstock from one and the headstock from another, and to bolt the two lathe beds in tandem atop a long support table.

Yet even though they have the means, no one in Mobile regularly turns full-length posts. Instead, area bedmakers have developed methods to join posts turned in shorter sections. These ideas can be used by any turner to join long work such as standing lamps and coat racks as well as bedposts. If you begin with full-length stock, as most bedmakers in Mobile do, you can make the grain in the finished work match from section to section. Yet this isn't absolutely necessary. Shorter stock may be much more available—and economical—and there is usually so much decoration around the joints that the continuity of the wood grain will be somewhat obscured in any case. A big advantage to working in sections is that your present lathe will probably be up to the job. Also, a post turned in sections will turn out straighter than a one-piece post.

The Reid shop rips post stock full length from 4-in. thick planks, and a typical blank will warp a little as it is cut from the

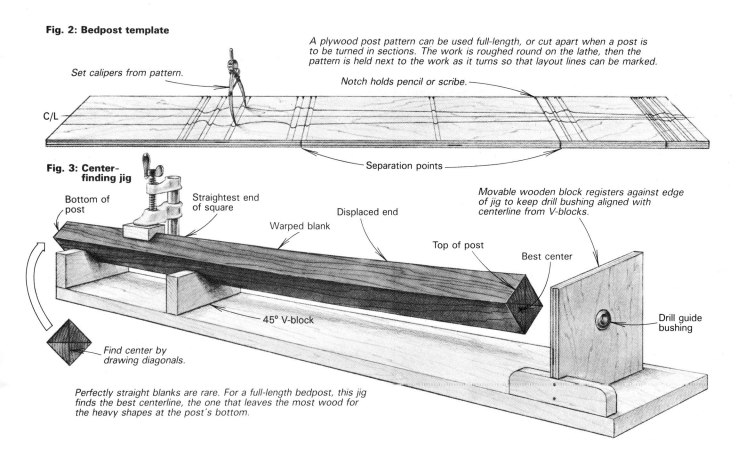

Fig. 2: Bedpost template

A plywood post pattern can be used full-length, or cut apart when a post is to be turned in sections. The work is roughed round on the lathe, then the pattern is held next to the work as it turns so that layout lines can be marked.

Set calipers from pattern.

Notch holds pencil or scribe.

C/L

Separation points

Fig. 3: Center-finding jig

Bottom of post

Straightest end of square

Displaced end

Warped blank

Movable wooden block registers against edge of jig to keep drill bushing aligned with centerline from V-blocks.

Top of post

Best center

Drill guide bushing

45° V-block

Find center by drawing diagonals.

Perfectly straight blanks are rare. For a full-length bedpost, this jig finds the best centerline, the one that leaves the most wood for the heavy shapes at the post's bottom.

board. If you are planning to cut a post into three or four sections, warp will not be too much of a problem, because you can square up the joints on the lathe, undercutting the endgrain a little for a perfect fit.

When working in sections, it's wise to consider which part of the joint should be tenon and which part mortise. There are often deep cove cuts either immediately above or below a joint, and the rule is to bore the mortise through what will be the heavier part in the finished post. It is a good idea to keep any joint mortises well away from the square mortises for the bed rails, in order not to weaken the post at this critical point. Bedposts typically separate as shown in figure 1, and an average tenon might be 1-in. to 1¼-in. dia., and about 3 in. long. Tenons are grooved to allow glue squeeze-out.

A crucial step in making a bedpost is to draw this sort of information, including the separation points, on a full length plywood pattern of the post, as shown in figure 2. If the post is to be turned in sections, the pattern can be cut apart and used to scribe separation points onto the stock, allowing extra length for integral tenons (at upper joints, where strength is not so critical, it is often possible to substitute a dowel, which conserves post stock and makes for better grain matching).

With the work in the lathe, hold the pattern next to it for marking the points where the profiles change. At the base of the post, and with the lathe turned off, mark the point where the square section ends, and scribe the lines around all four faces. Then round off the corners with the point of a skew chisel. Mark the other points on the work after it has been roughed round with a gouge—simply hold the pattern next to the stock as it turns and slide a pencil down the notch in the pattern. Then set calipers according to the pattern and transfer the di-

ameters to the work with a parting tool.

If you cut full-length stock into sections, be sure to mark their orientation on the end grain as soon as you cut the divisions, so that they can be turned and assembled in the correct order. You can mark the matching sections A (for the bottom of the post), then B-B, C-C, etc. These letters will serve to keep you from accidentally reversing a section when you put it in the lathe. These marks will probably be turned away when you square up the joint lines, but you can mark them again at that time so you won't intermix post sections later.

If you have a long-bed lathe and decide to have few separation points in your design, you will have to consider how much the stock is warped. In ordinary turning, a slightly warped piece of wood is simply center-marked at both ends, and the warp is turned away. But in a bedpost, such a procedure may cause problems. It is necessary for the square section of the stock to stand straight and to be perpendicular to the bed rails. This means that the blank must be chucked in the lathe with the square part of the post on-center—any warp in the blank must be confined to the length of the post that will be above the rails. Figure 3 shows a jig that finds the best centers for a full length post. The bottom of the post (the straightest end of the blank) is marked with diagonals to show its center, then is held in a pair of V-blocks. The warped end is allowed to go its own way. A movable wooden block with a drill-guide bushing in it then locates the "center" at the final end. If you make a jig like this, locate the drill-guide bushing in the block according to the size of the V-blocks and the stock. To check that the bushing is correct, put the block at the base of the post (the end that will remain square); the bushing must align exactly with the marked center. Of course in stock that is too badly warped, you may not

Robert Reid gauges a bedpost tenon to the right diameter, using calipers and a parting tool at several places along its length.

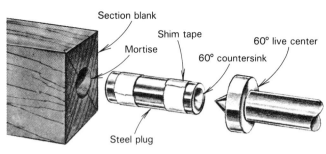

Section blank

Shim tape

Mortise

60° countersink

60° live center

Steel plug

Tenons are turned on the lathe, which ensures that they are perfectly centered and parallel to the section's centerline. Mortises are bored in the square stock, then the post section is turned using a plug in the mortise to ensure that the post is centered around it.

Fig. 5: Bandsaw taper jig

This bandsaw jig can taper a full-length octagonal post. It can also remove excess wood from a blank before turning. The head block indexes the top of the post in the finial-pin mortise (drilled as shown in figure 3), while the base of the post is supported by a block that is sized to register against either the flat sides or the corners, allowing the blank to be rotated for successive cuts.

Detail: Cutting sequence

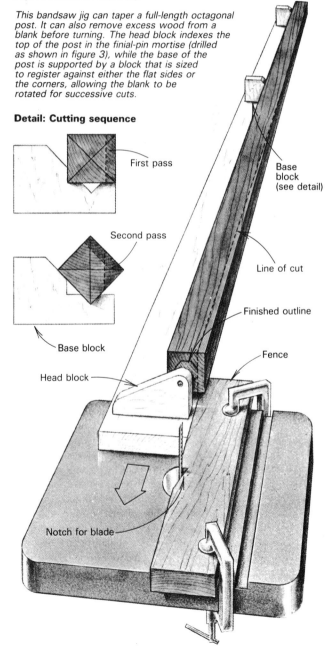

First pass

Second pass

Base block

Base block (see detail)

Line of cut

Finished outline

Fence

Head block

Notch for blade

be able to turn full length without running out of wood.

When the finial center has been drilled, the blank is usually divided into two sections before turning. Because the tenon is turned at the top of the square section of the post, the upper post section must have a mortise at its bottom end as well as one for the finial pin. It is no trick to center a turned tenon, but it would be almost impossible to accurately center the matching mortise if it were drilled after the stock had been turned. The solution is to bore the mortise before turning, then insert a steel plug in the hole, as shown in figure 4. One end of the plug is countersunk to match the 60° live center at the tailstock, which centers the pre-drilled mortise so that the post can be turned around it. When mounting the work in the lathe, the finial end goes at the head-stock, and is driven by a spur center that instead of having a point, has a center pin that fits the finial mortise. Both mortises, therefore, end up centered in the post.

The center-finding jig is also useful if you plan to make a pen-cil post bed, one with octagonal posts instead of turned ones. When the Reids make a pencil post, they first find the center and drill the hole for the finial pin, then they mount the blank on a sliding jig that runs past a commercial shaper, which cuts each face of the tapered octagon in turn. Robert Reid got the basic idea from Roy Blake, whose original jig worked on the bandsaw, as shown in figure 5. The jig indexes the finial mortise on a pin that allows the post to be rotated for successive cuts. The band-saw blade cuts a straight taper from the top of the post, but the taper ends above the square base of the post. Thus, the bottom of the post can be used to index each cut in turn, by resting first on a flat face and then on a corner. In order that the taper end grace-fully, the corner cuts must be stopped before the blade exits the work. The blade is then backed out of the cut and the waste

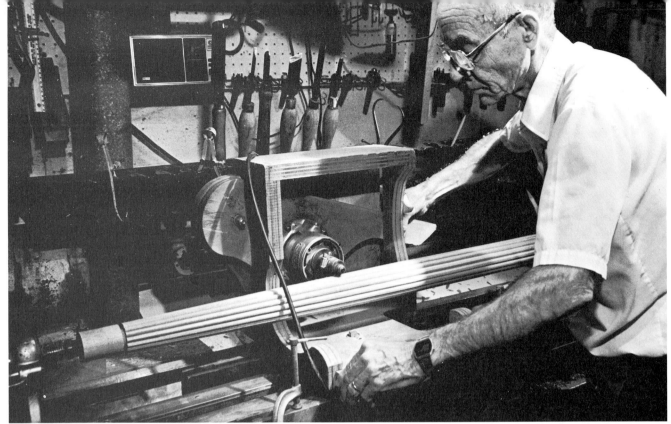

Julian Reid, above, operates a reeding jig—a carriage that rolls along the lathe ways carrying a router mounted on a pivoting arm. A bearing on the bit holder follows the contours of the work, which is locked in position by an indexing plate at the headstock. Mobile bedmaker William Blake, left, demonstrates his similar jig, which uses a simpler solid-pilot bit machined from tool steel (far left). The setscrew visible at the end of the bit locks the V-shaped cutter in place.

Reid's ingenious rope-twist machine, shown below, uses a bit similar to the straight-reeding machine (top), but in this case the carriage is attached to a cable arrangement that hooks up to the headstock spindle. As the operator moves the carriage along the ways, the work rotates a specific, adjustable amount for each inch the carriage moves.

Robert Reid's shopmade duplicating router carves four knees at once, following a pattern mounted in the center.

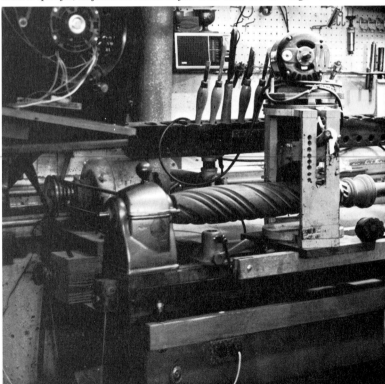

The Reid shop shapes lamb's tongues on a pencil-post by pattern-sanding the curves on a belt-sander.

Fig. 6: Aligning multiple-dowel joints

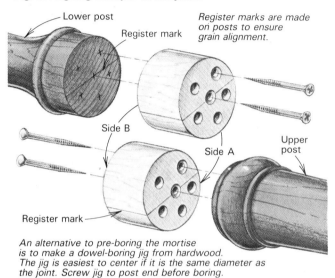

Lower post

Register mark

Register marks are made on posts to ensure grain alignment.

Side B

Side A

Upper post

Register mark

An alternative to pre-boring the mortise is to make a dowel-boring jig from hardwood. The jig is easiest to center if it is the same diameter as the joint. Screw jig to post end before boring.

A bed with cabriole legs must have unusually heavy corner posts to withstand the strain put upon the rails. Note that this section of the post carries the tenon. If the tenon were on the upper section, the corner post would have to be mortised, weakening the construction.

nipped off, leaving enough wood for either a lamb's tongue or a simple cove. The Reid shop makes lamb's tongues by pattern-sanding, as shown in the top photo on this page. Lamb's tongues can also be shaped by hand with spokeshaves, carving tools or drum sanders in an electric drill. The tapered faces can be cleaned up with a few strokes of a plane.

An alternative method for aligning sections of a post is shown in figure 6. The joint is held together by four dowels, which are accurately located by means of a hardwood boring jig screwed to the end of the section. The jig is easiest to center if it is made the same diameter as the finished post. Grain alignment is accomplished by registering the jig on reference lines marked on the stock before it is turned. Posts can be clamped up by jacking them against a ceiling joist or by building an extra long clamp.

The jigs shown thus far are enough to make several authentic bedpost designs. But fancy ones call for reeding, fluting, carving and other decorations. In the old days, these chores were done by hand, but Robert Reid quickly found that handwork was too costly, and he soon invented some production methods. As he says: "Any time a machine can make a perfect duplicate of handwork, a man would be foolish to insist on doing the job by hand. But a 100% machine-produced object that arrives at only a 98% duplication of handwork is a compromise with integrity. What you want is whatever the machine can do—25%, 75%, 98%—plus whatever handwork it takes to finish the job right."

The four-man Reid shop can turn out about 125 beds a year, each one taking about two weeks through the system. Every bed is a custom order—the shop will make any combination of posts, headboard and tester. Machines do most of the roughing out, but the final touches still require handwork. There's a duplicating lathe, for example, that follows a pattern with four ounces of pressure on its stylus, and applies 400 pounds of pressure to cut the wood. The bedpost comes off the lathe clean enough that a lot of factories would then simply sand, stain and lacquer it, but Reid's remounts the work on another lathe and refines the shapes by hand-turning.

Similarly, Reid built a router jig, shown in the top photo on the facing page, for reeding bedposts. The work is locked in position by an indexing plate at the headstock. Then the carriage is moved along the lathe bed by hand, and a router mounted on a pivoting arm follows the contours of the work, piloted by the bit holder. Reid's uses a commercial bit holder, with a ½-in. shank and ball-bearing pilot. Bedmaker William Blake has adapted the idea using a bit machined from steel, with the cutter held in place by a setscrew from the end. Blake's cutter and jig are shown in the photos at far left on the facing page.

Reid also built a duplicating router (bottom left, facing page) that follows a carved leg and makes four simultaneous copies. These also get their share of hand carving before stain and lacquer go on. One of Reid's most ingenious machines (left, center) looks like a great-granddaddy of the Sears Router-Crafter. It's a router setup that makes helical rope-twist bedposts, and he cobbled it up from Model-A parts when he was only nineteen years old. Reid recalls the first Victorian rope-twist bed he made: "I had to carve each post by hand, and it seemed like I would never finish. If there's an easier way to do something, I'm going to do my best to uncover it." But it's a safe bet that he's not going to lower his standards to do so. □

Asher Carmichael works for Emperor Clock Co., in Fairhope, Ala. Photos on pages 30 and 31 (except photo at far left, bottom of page 30) by the author.

The Louisville Slugger
Custom-turned bats for baseball's heavy hitters

by Paul Bertorelli

A major league bat must be within an ounce of the weight specified by the player who will use it.

When I played sandlot baseball, I devised the cleverest batting strategy that my childhood grasp of physics would allow I grabbed the biggest bat in the box, reasoning that no pitcher could possibly throw a ball past such a fat target held anywhere near the strike zone.

Until I visited the Louisville Slugger baseball bat factory, I hadn't connected my abysmal batting average with the trouble I had swinging those monsters off my shoulder before the ball whizzed by At the famous Slugger plant, I learned that hitting is the end product of a refined equation in which four guys standing at lathes figure prominently. I'd read about how big-league bats are custom-turned for each player, so I went to see how it's done.

The Slugger factory—known properly as the Hillerich and Bradsby Co.—is actually not in Louisville at all but across the Ohio River in Jeffersonville, Ind. They've been making bats in the Louisville area since 1884, when the founder's son, Bud Hillerich, took to turning them for a local ball team in his father's job-shop turnery. Players found Hillerich's bats to be a great improvement over the crude, shapeless clubs they'd been accustomed to, and by the turn of the century, H&B was established as the premier maker of major league bats.

My tour of the plant began with a walk through the timber yard, where thousands of 3-in. by 40-in. white ash billets are left to air-dry. High tensile strength, resiliency and, most of all, lightness make ash the preferred bat wood, though hickory has also been used. Rex Bradley, H&B's timber and professional-bat expert, told me that the billets are shipped in from seven mills situated along the Pennsylvania-New York border, where soil and climate conditions encourage the moderately fast growth rates that result in ideal bat timber. Fast-growth timber is avoided because its greater ratio of dense latewood makes the same size billet heavier, giving hand-turners less leeway in matching size and weight.

The billets are dried to about 10% moisture content, rough-turned, and sorted by weight and quality. The best will become major league bats; the rest softball and adult league models, the vast majority of the million or so wooden bats that H&B turns every year. As you would expect, the bat factory is a noisy place, with most of the floor given over to ranks of squat, semi-automatic lathes that spin out bats as fast as workers can load in blanks. Off in one corner, away from the din, was what I had come to see: the hand lathes and four turners who together make 20,000 major league bats a year.

Each bat is custom-turned to suit the swing, grip and whims of the player who will wield it. Bill Williams, an H&B vice president, told me that modern players prefer lighter, shorter bats over the heavy clubs I thought were the key to hot hitting. "Babe Ruth used a 42-ounce bat," Williams said. "You don't see any that heavy today. Most of the bats we make are around 32 to 35 ounces." That's because modern players face a more cunning variety of pitches than did their predecessors.

In Ruth's day, a batter might have faced the same pitcher three or four times in one game. By the end of the day, he would have seen enough of the pitcher's tricks to adjust his swing accordingly. Today's player has to contend with a starting pitcher and any number of relievers, each one with a different curve, fastball and slider. Because it can be snapped more quickly, a lighter bat allows the hitter to scope the approaching pitch an instant longer before he decides to swing, thus increasing his odds for a hit. The batmaker's challenge is to shave off as much wood as he can without weakening the bat's slender handle.

I watched Freeman Young turn a bat for Mike Jorgensen, a New York Mets utility fielder. Jorgensen likes a 32-oz. bat that's 35 in. long, requiring Young to skim the handle down to near its breaking point. Young picked a blank from racks sorted by weight, chucked it in his lathe and went to work. His toolkit is sparse: three gouges, a knob-sizing tool, and a yardstick with a knife in one end to mark the bat's length. With a 1¼-in. gouge, Young roughed the shape by eyeballing a bat he took from H&B's artifact room, where a sample of each of the hundreds of past and present models is kept. If no model exists, the turner looks up a card on each player that describes the diameter of his bat at 15 points along its length. He turns those diameters, checking with a caliper, then connects the points with a fair curve.

"I like to do the knob and the handle first," Young said, after he slid his gouge along the lathe's long, continuous tool

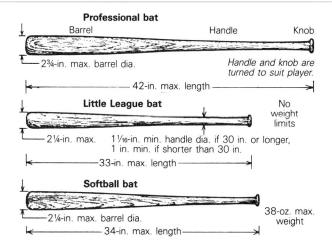

Professional bat

Barrel · · · Handle · · · Knob

2¾-in. max. barrel dia.

Handle and knob are turned to suit player.

42-in. max. length

Little League bat

No weight limits

2¼-in. max. · · · 1¹⁄₁₆-in. min. handle dia. if 30 in. or longer, 1 in. min. if shorter than 30 in.

33-in. max. length

Softball bat

2¼-in. max. barrel dia.

38-oz. max. weight

34-in. max. length

rest. "That way if it breaks, I won't have wasted my time on the barrel." Other H&B turners do just the opposite, figuring that turning the barrel first reduces the blank's weight, minimizing whip and reducing the risk of breakage. Young set his sizing tool a bit larger than the model's knob diameter. The extra material is needed because the sizing tool's high angle of attack scrapes rather than cuts, leaving a rough, cratered surface. Young smoothed the knob to size with a ½-in. gouge. He switched back to a larger gouge to slim the handle and lower barrel, lubricating the tool's travel along the rest with an occasional swipe of an oily rag. As he neared the finished size, Young checked his bat against the model by lining up his caliper with a position marker consisting of a steel rod that slides along another rod mounted behind the lathe and parallel to its centers.

I could see the bat flex as the tool cut the narrowest part of the handle, but before it began to whip, Young hooked his callused left hand behind the spinning work to support it. Oddly, the turners here had never heard of bracing slender work with a steady rest. I doubt they would use one anyway. They have to hustle to make their daily quota of 32 bats, and a steady would just slow them down.

Once Young had duplicated the model, he turned down both ends with a parting tool, gave the new bat a once-over with rough sandpaper and tossed it onto a scale above his lathe. It weighed 32½ oz. "I like to get 'em right on...an ounce either way is okay for the major leagues," Young said. Final-sanding, finishing (lacquer) and the famous Slugger burned-in brand happen in another part of the plant. In the 10 minutes that had elapsed between centering the blank and weigh-in, Young hadn't stopped his lathe, neither to remove the completed bat nor to chuck a fresh blank.

Watching Young work, I realized that turning a bat is easy compared to the arcane task of selecting the right timber. "Ballplayers are notoriously superstitious about their bats," Bradley, a one-time minor leaguer himself, told me. "Ruth liked to have pin knots up around the barrel, Pete Rose won't use anything but wide-growth ash. To us, timber is timber, but we try to give a player what he wants so he won't have any doubt in his mind when he steps up to the plate." Some players even visit the plant to supervise the turning, having a little removed here and there until the balance is just so.

This infinite adjustability has, in part, kept wooden Sluggers from being driven to extinction by aluminum bats, the weapon of choice in Little League and college baseball. Aluminum bats can't be tailored to each player, but the metal is arguably a better bat material than wood. For its weight, it's stronger than ash, and it never has wind shakes or worm holes. Weak hitters do better with aluminum because the metal bats have a larger "sweet spot," that area of the barrel which imparts the most power when it strikes the ball squarely.

Tradition, however, is likely to have more to say about the survival of wooden bats in the majors than any volume of debate over how well they work or don't work. "It really comes down to pleasing the ballpark crowd," said Williams. "An aluminum bat just can't match the sound that a wooden bat makes when it hits the ball." □

Hillerich and Bradsby offers tours of its plant and baseball museum. For more information, write the company at PO Box 35700, Louisville, Ky. 40232. Paul Bertorelli is editor of Fine Woodworking *magazine.*

Four woodworkers at H&B hand-turn most of the bats swung by major league players. To make a bat for a particular player, the turner duplicates one of the hundreds of current models filed in the artifact room, above.

Above, turner Freeman Young sets his sizing tool to the model bat's knob diameter. He'll size the knob on the new bat and then shape it with a small gouge.

To keep the slender handle of a light bat from breaking, Young steadies the spinning work by hooking his left hand behind it. The thumb presses the gouge to the tool rest, ensuring a precise shearing cut that leaves a smooth surface.

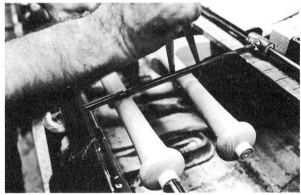

As he turns a new bat to near its final size, Young checks his work against the model with calipers. He aligns the measuring instrument via a position marker that slides along a steel rod mounted behind the lathe and parallel to its centers.

Spinning Wheels

The tricky parts are the flyer/bobbin and the wheel itself

by Bud Kronenberg

One of the most compelling motivations for working with wood is the natural urge to create. When we successfully produce an item that is well-built, useful and good-looking, our feelings of pride and achievement are temporarily satisfied. However, I don't think a woodworker has realized the fullest sense of achievement until he or she makes a thing that is not only functional and beautiful, but also works mechanically and productively, such as a spinning wheel.

There are two broad categories of spinning wheels. The large "walking" wheel (so named because the spinner has to walk to operate it) is used for spinning wool. The wheel is from 3 ft. to 6 ft. in diameter, and its rim is 1½ in. to 4 in. wide. The spindle is turned by a drive band on wheels of different sizes. A walking wheel, however, requires one operation to spin the fiber and another to store the yarn. The second category includes treadle wheels, originally used to spin flax into linen and modified in the late 1800s to spin both flax and wool. The key to this "modern" wheel is the flyer/bobbin, invented by Leonardo da Vinci about the time Columbus discovered America, which spins and stores the

yarn in one continuous motion. In 1530 Johann Jurgen, a German from Saxony, developed a treadle arrangement to activate da Vinci's device. Thus treadle wheels are also known as Saxony wheels.

The purpose of a spinning wheel—or any other spinning device—is to twist short individual fibers into an overlapping long thread, which can then be woven into cloth. Most animal fibers, and many plant fibers, have microscopic teeth that engage each other when the fibers are twisted together. This interlocking is what makes a spun fiber strong and suitable for weaving. On the Saxony wheel, the fibers are twisted as they pass through the orifice, the hole in the end of the shaft. The resulting yarn or thread passes over the hooks on the flyer and onto the bobbin for storage. Since the bobbin must revolve faster than the flyer in order to pull the yarn through the orifice, the bobbin pulley diameter is usually ¼ in. to ½ in. smaller than that of the whorl pulley that moves the flyer. Pulley diameters can be changed to suit yarn thickness. Increasing the sizes of both pulleys makes for slower spinning, an advantage for beginners who haven't yet

From *Fine Woodworking* magazine (Summer 1978) 11:40-46

Anatomy of a Saxony Wheel

Dimensions and details are taken from author's Shaker-style wheel, shown in photo at left.

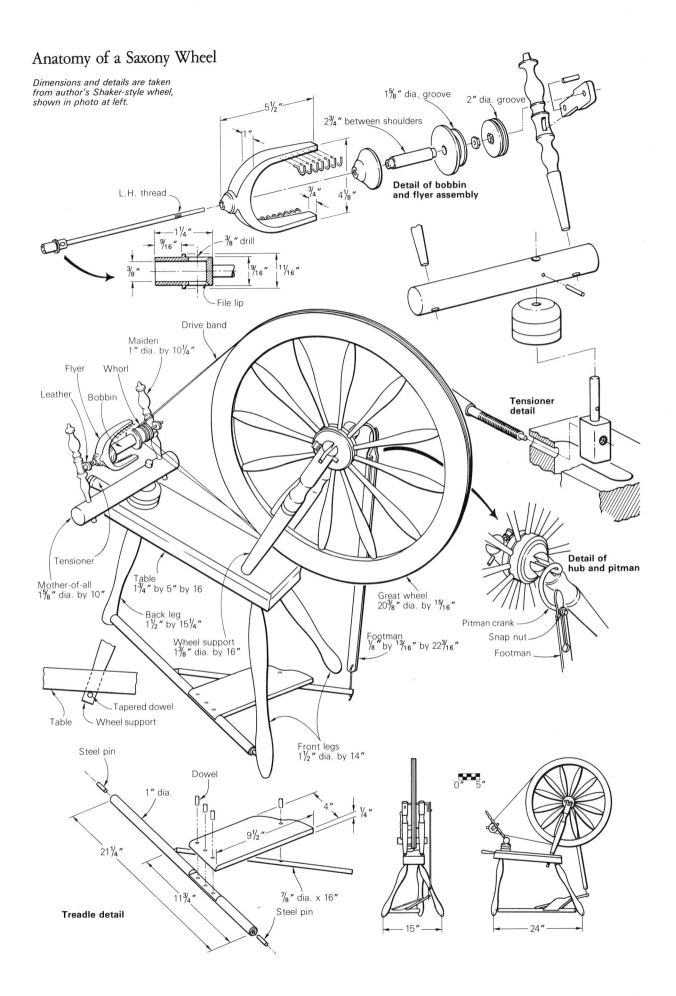

5½"

1"

2¾" between shoulders

1⅝" dia. groove

2" dia. groove

Detail of bobbin and flyer assembly

L.H. thread

¾"

4⅛"

1¼"

9/16"

⅜" drill

⅜"

9/16"

11/16"

File lip

Drive band

Maiden
1" dia. by 10¼"

Whorl

Flyer

Leather

Bobbin

Tensioner detail

Tensioner

Mother-of-all
1⅝" dia. by 10"

Table
1¾" by 5" by 16

Back leg
1½" by 15¼"

Wheel support
1⅜" dia. by 16"

Great wheel
20⅜" dia. by 15/16"

Footman
⅛" by 13/16" by 22³/16"

Detail of hub and pitman

Pitman crank

Snap nut

Footman

Tapered dowel

Table

Wheel support

Front legs
1½" dia. by 14"

Steel pin

Dowel

1" dia.

4"

¼"

9½"

21¼"

11¾"

⅞" dia. x 16"

Steel pin

Treadle detail

0" 5"

15"

24"

Left, 'walking' wheel has no treadle and is spun by hand. It is used for heavy fibers and thick yarns. Center, two-handed 'gossip,' or 'courting,' wheel (c. 1875), designed to increase production. Right, early 19th-century chair wheel has two wheels connected by a drive band, for high speed. Double treadle and pitman permit precise starts and stops without hand propelling.

got the knack of feeding in the fibers smoothly and rapidly.

To use a Saxony wheel, one first ties a leader of yarn to the bobbin and threads it back over all the flyer hooks and through the orifice. Then the spinner feeds in the prepared and roughly aligned fibers and works the foot treadle. The impetus of the treadle is transmitted to the flyer and bobbin via a double drive band around the great wheel. The spinner moves the yarn back and forth from hook to hook on the flyer so that the yarn winds evenly onto the bobbin. When the bobbin is full it is removed, and another is inserted.

When I began making spinning wheels, the only electric equipment I had was a lathe, a drill and a sabre saw. Despite laboring 60 hours on each wheel, they were not the epitome of workmanship or workability. You don't need elaborate equipment, but you do have to think and plan ahead. I've added a band saw, wood threading kit, circular saw, radial drill press, and router and table. Now I spend about 15 hours on a medium-sized wheel—complete. The equipment has helped to reduce the time, but more important are experience and the jigs I've had to concoct.

Our primary attention will be focused on the treadle wheel, because it's the most popular with today's spinners. If you can make a treadle wheel, you'll have little difficulty making the simpler wool wheel. Even the rim of the large wool wheel is easy, because you don't have to steam the ¼-in. oak to bend it into a circle 5 or 6 feet in diameter. I've done this with ¼-in. oak 200 years old without soaking or steaming, and without any sign of impending casualty.

You can take working measurements from an antique wheel, but the exercise of measuring a few of them will prove to you that nothing is standard about them. All the dimensions and the design of each turning are different from wheel to wheel, although each builder had preferences that appear in much of his work—this we know because many of the makers signed their wheels. There are some critical relationships which must be maintained if the wheel is to spin properly, and I've tried to discuss them as they arise in the text and diagrams. The dimensions given here are taken from my reproduction of a Shaker-style wheel. There isn't anything magic about them, except that they work.

If you do intend to reproduce an old wheel, the turnings should all be of the same design, but you don't have to match the ones on your model. There are hundreds of styles of an-

tique wheels. Take your pick from the highly ornamental ones found in the Philadelphia area, down to the very plain Shaker style. The Irish preferred the upright type, East Europeans favored very small wheels—sometimes only 20 in. from floor to top—the French liked decorative turnings, and so on.

Materials

I've made wheels from pine, walnut, maple, oak and cherry. In my opinion, pine is too light; maple is nice to work but hard to color properly; oak is good for rims and tables; walnut is expensive and I don't like its dirt-like dust. Unlike others, I have had good luck threading walnut. But my favorite is black cherry. The natural coloring is beautiful, and it's fine for all parts of the wheel. All the material for a Saxony wheel should cost less than $20 (1978 prices throughout).

To be historically authentic, use thoroughly dry white or red oak for the rim and the table. If you demand complete authenticity, you'll use only quartersawn oak, as the Colonists did. You'll probably use less wood than you thought you'd need. That's because there are so many small parts to use up the small leftovers. I cut the rim from full 1-in. stock and square up the quartermoon leftovers for spokes.

Wheel

The most difficult part to construct is the wheel itself. It requires the most accuracy, because it must be flat, true and perfectly round. When you have a good wheel, the rest of the job will be fairly simple. I sell wheels only for $65, and a complete spinning wheel for as little as $125. This shows the importance I put on the wheel. It's not the materials, it's the time it takes to fit and assemble. It takes me only about 10 minutes to turn a spoke. My wheels have from 4 to 20 spokes, depending on the style. It is almost always an even number, which gives the best balance and design.

The first step is to make a template of the rim to the specified width (from 1½ in. to 4 in.). This is nothing more than two perfect circles drawn on the template material of your choice—Masonite or cardboard is fine. Quarter the circle as shown in the drawing (opposite page), and transfer the four sections to the wood, running the grain lengthwise. Cut the sections as squarely as possible and use every bit of skill you can muster for the inside cutting of the circle. Don't be overly concerned with the outside, because it will be recut later. In fact, some makers leave the outside square for now, as the straight edges can help in getting the joints to fit truly.

The four joints can be blind mortise and tenon, splined, or doweled. I've found it necessary to work on a perfectly flat surface. When I started out, there wasn't such a thing in my workshop—so I tried a piece of plate glass large enough to accommodate the entire wheel. Not only is the glass flat, but you can hold it up to inspect the progress of the joints from below. When that's done you can get ready to put the joints together, using the best glue you know of. I use one pipe clamp with a thickness of waxed paper over the plate glass to prevent sticking (and spoiling my only flat surface). When putting pressure on with the clamp, which is on each of the two longest rim sections, be careful the joints don't buckle up—not a fraction. It's better to back off on the clamp if the work leaves the glass. If you're using a doweled joint, let the glue set, then drill and dowel with one or two dowels through the outside of the rim, but not all the way through. Vee-groove the dowels for better glue contact.

While the rim is setting, I turn the hub of the wheel. Before you take it off the lathe, put a circumferential cut mark in the exact center of the rim of the hub as you face it, spinning on the lathe. This is important and will save frustration later on. After the hub is sanded and polished you're ready to drill the spoke holes. Mine are usually ⅜ in., but follow your own measurements. Instead of trusting to my error-prone math to space the spoke holes, I make a pencil mark on the cut-line to use as a starting point, and work with dividers through trial and error until I get the spacing correct. After the spoke holes are drilled, put a witness mark across the center line, and cut the hub in half along the circumferential center cut. I've found this "split-hub" method makes the strongest wheel, but there is another method I'll explain later. Don't drill the axle hole yet.

Before you start making the spokes, measure the diameter of the holes in the hub, because you've reduced them by the thickness of the kerf when you cut it in half. I make my spokes freehand, with the aid of calipers. I don't have a duplicating attachment for my lathe, but I soothe my feelings by telling myself, neither did the American settlers. When I am bored by the repetition of many spokes, I do a couple of them on my 100-year-old foot-treadle lathe. Promptly, my respect for the early craftsman zooms.

The inside of the wheel rim must be just as round as you can get it, and now is the time to sand and shape it if you're going to, because soon the spokes will be in place. I use a large-diameter sanding drum on the drill press. Locate the spoke holes using my stupid method or your superior math. With the rim together, chances are your drill press will not fit inside to drill the holes. I've found that I can be accurate enough with a simple drill jig and an electric hand-drill. If you're making a very small wheel, you may have to hack a few inches off your bit to get the drill inside the rim.

The best time to start assembling the wheel is on a quiet evening when you won't be interrupted—there's no stopping once you start. The hub must be centered as perfectly as possible, laterally and longitudinally, with the inside of the rim. The cut surface of the hub must be in the center of the thickness of the rim. Not an easy task, but you can do it by using shims and being careful. Take time to experiment. Put the spokes in the rim, lay them on one half of the hub and put the other half on top. By holding them together you should

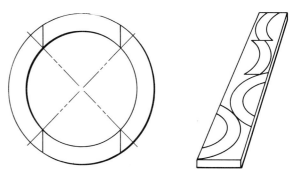

Quarter the wheel template, then lay out the four segments on a 1-in. plank. The waste crescents may be squared up and turned for spokes.

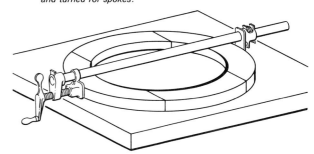

Use a single bar clamp to butt-glue the four segments together; working on plate glass ensures flatness.

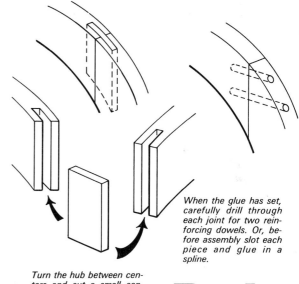

When the glue has set, carefully drill through each joint for two reinforcing dowels. Or, before assembly slot each piece and glue in a spline.

Turn the hub between centers and cut a small centered notch around the circumference.

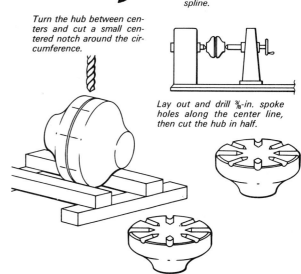

Lay out and drill ⅜-in. spoke holes along the center line, then cut the hub in half.

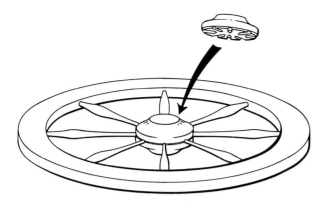

Center the half-hub in the rim, place the spokes, and put the other half-hub on top. Don't glue until everything is just right.

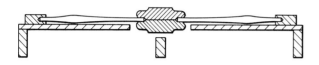

A shallow box with a center hole (shown in section) allows the hub and rim to sit flat for drilling the axle hole. For alternate assembly method, shown below, drill spoke holes in solid hub and rabbet inside of rim, then notch spoke ends to fit rabbet shoulder. Pin with small dowels.

be able to pick up the wheel in one hand. When you have the situation under control, glue the spokes in the rim and turn them so the best grain shows. Apply glue to the bottom half of the hub, then to the spoke ends and the top half of the hub and clamp. I stress accuracy in locating the hub, but you'll still have a chance to make a slight correction when drilling the axle hole. Remember, the perimeter of the wheel still hasn't been rounded out yet.

The next step is locating the axle hole, by repeated measurement from the inside of the rim. Drill the axle hole and be sure that it is exactly perpendicular to the rim. The jig shown above, which I call a "wheel-box," will help situate the wheel perpendicular to the drill-press bit. The diameter of the axle hole depends on the size of the axle and the method you use to secure the axle to the hub.

The alternative method to drilling spoke holes in the rim is to rout a ¼-in. rabbet on the inside of the rim, down to about three-quarters of its thickness. The spokes fit holes drilled in the hub and are notched to fit over the remaining shoulder at the rim, then pinned with ⅛-in. hardwood dowel angled through the rim from the lip side. This ancient method uses no glue. Its advantage is that you can adjust the trueness of the wheel by moving the spokes across the thickness of the rim. I've done it this way, but prefer the split hub because I believe modern glues make it stronger. However, wheels constructed by rim-rabbeting have lasted for hundreds of years. If you're after authenticity, this is the way to do it.

Now we need an axle and pitman crank. This caused me

problems at first, because there's a surprising torque and strain on the axle and hub. The axle can't be allowed to turn or slip in the hub. The old-timers solved the problem by making a square hole in the hub, and squaring the axle part that passed through it. I find it difficult to make square holes and I don't if I don't have to, so I use regular hardware-store ¼-in. steel rod and weld a washer to it. Then I drill four holes in the washer and brad the washer to the hub. This makes it possible to take the wheel apart if need be. You're not ready, at this point, to fasten the axle permanently to the wheel— don't. First you have to make the outside of the rim perfectly round. The jig shown on the next page is the best way I know to do this. Use a rod as a pivot to turn the wheel into your band saw. Bear in mind that the pivot should be even with the blade. If you don't have a band saw, you can put a 90° bend in a rod that will fit your sabre saw or router. With the rod in the axle hole and the sabre saw on the other end, you can cut the circle and make out pretty well.

The perfected outside rim must now be grooved to take the drive band. You can make two V-shaped grooves, or one wide groove with straight shoulders. Make them deep enough—at least ¼ in., and preferably ⁵⁄₁₆ in. Old wheels were grooved both ways, and either way spins equally well. Without a router or shaper, you're in for a lot of work with a rabbet plane, file and rasp, unless you can concoct a way of mounting the wheel outboard on the lathe. After grooving, you may want to do some decorative routing on the flat side of the rim. I do this using the same method I suggested for sabre-sawing the outside rim: With a rod in the axle hole, I swing the router around the wheel. This works very well and quickly. Don't make the decorative grooves too deep; ¹⁄₁₆ in. is usually sufficient.

The table

Next I start on the table using 2-in. planed, or full 8/4 stock, 6 in. to 8 in. wide. Some tables are slightly tapered toward the end with the tension device. A half-inch off each side is plenty of taper. The top of the table will be very visible, so choose wood with attractive figure. The reverse is true of the underside—it will seldom be seen. Just be sure it doesn't have knots that would interfere with the holes you'll be drilling later. At this stage do some preliminary sanding and any design shaping you wish.

The three legs are next. Turn them from the 2-in. stock, making the two front legs the same length and the back leg an inch or two longer if your table is sloping. Drilling the leg holes in the table can be tricky because the angles must be exact. My solution is a radial drill press. A riskier method is a hand-held bit and brace guided by sighting a sliding bevel. The legs have to be a tight drive fit into the table. You can get a good fit by careful tapering on the lathe, and by reaming the leg hole. Don't drive the legs in yet, because you're going to have to take them out again before you're through.

The next step is the two wheel-support uprights. They too will be a tight drive fit. Take pains to drill the support holes particularly accurately—they must be parallel. If they're not, the wheel will go off at an angle and you'll always have an unsatisfactory spinner. The axle slots in the supports are also critical. Both should be the same depth when the supports are seated, so a rod set in the slots is parallel to the table. Now you can see how your wheel is going to look. Using a rod or dowel, put the wheel in place. Spin it slowly. Is it running true? Don't worry if it rubs on one side, because later it will be riding on leather bearings that can be built up on one side more than the other to compensate for the tilt. Don't ever glue the upright supports into the table. If you don't have a tight fit, save yourself later grief and make new supports now.

After the wheel supports are in, we can finish making the axle and pitman, because we now know the distance between the outside of the wheel supports. To make the pitman crank, I fit a piece of pipe over the rod, for leverage. You may wish to heat it and pound out a better arc. As you look at the wheel from the pitman side, the curve goes counterclockwise, which means that from the spinner's side it goes clockwise. The end of the pitman fits a slot in the drive rod, or footman, so the turned-over tip should be long enough (about ½ in. to ¾ in.) to accept the footman and a snap-nut that holds it in place. Be sure the turned-over tip is parallel to the main axle.

Tension device

It's best to slot the table for the tension device before making the threaded parts. I've found it best to locate the slot about ½ in. off center toward the spinner's side. Drill a hole to accept your sabre saw or coping saw, then cut out the slot. In the end grain of the table, drill a hole to fit the tension screw, centered on the short dimension of the slot rectangle. This hole should be slightly below the center of the 2-in. thickness of the table. Just leave enough wood beneath it—½ in. or so. I prefer to make the diameter of the tension screws at least ¾ in. and 1 in. is better, with a ½-in. guide peg on the end. Drill a hole to receive the guide peg into the opposite end of the tension slot. Now turn the tension screw and thread it with a screwbox, or die.

Before I had threading tools, I used ½-in. threaded steel rod pinned into a turned handle. For the upright part that moves the mother-of-all, I welded a rod on the flat edge of a square nut. This works perfectly well and doesn't affect the appearance of the wheel because it's concealed.

The side walls of the tension slot have to be parallel and squared off, because the mother-of-all holder is going to travel its full length. If it is not accurately made, the holder with the female thread will bind on the sides. Turn the holder but leave a square section to drill and thread. The dowel part can be left longer than necessary and cut to length later. Turn the half-ball part that is directly beneath the mother-of-all. This is not attached, ever, to the upright from the tension screw. The mother-of-all and maidens are easily turned, but take care when drilling the holes for the maidens—they must be a tight force-fit. Notice that they angle back away from the wheel and are not perpendicular to the table. Cut both leather bearing slots in the maidens the same distance up from the mother-of-all. Don't put any of these parts together permanently, yet.

Treadle

The next step, if you're following my order of working, is to make the treadle bar, treadle platform and arm. If you want to be fancy, you can dovetail the platform into the treadle bar. This lends a pleasing touch. The simplest way to attach the platform is to have it ride on top of the bar and dowel it on, or you can mortise it. Now, we come to another operation that could lead to a pitfall, if care isn't taken. The hole in the end of the treadle arm must come directly beneath the pitman crank when it's in the down position. Put the wheel in

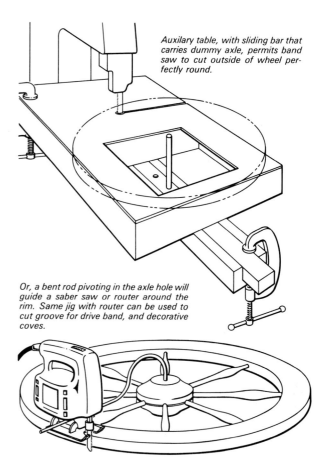

Auxilary table, with sliding bar that carries dummy axle, permits band saw to cut outside of wheel perfectly round.

Or, a bent rod pivoting in the axle hole will guide a saber saw or router around the rim. Same jig with router can be used to cut groove for drive band, and decorative coves.

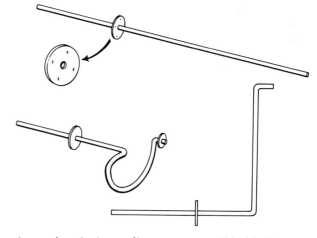

The pitman-crank axle is made from ¼-in. rod with a washer welded to it. Make the bends in the sequence shown, taking distances from your wheel and uprights.

place and angle the treadle arm to accomplish this. You can now drill the angled hole in the bar to accept the treadle arm. Use cut-off spikes, or rod, for the metal pins on each end of the treadle bar. The pins should come straight out of the ends of the bar. These pins will go into holes in the one front leg nearest the spinner, and in the back leg. You have to remove the legs to install the treadle.

If you want to try out the treadle action, make the footman and put the wheel in place with strips of leather in the bottom of the slots for bearings. Chances are you'll find the wheel jumps up and down as you treadle. Center the wheel between the uprights by adding or subtracting thicknesses of bearing leather, then drill a ¼-in. hole just above the axle, all the way through the upright nearest the spinner, and turn a peg to fit. This will hold the axle in place and stop the jumping. In actual use, the bearing leathers will be oiled continuously, but if you oil them now you may affect the finish.

The flyer and bobbin

You can purchase an excellent flyer-bobbin assembly for about $30 (1978 price). A good source is Eric Gudat, 460 Union St., Washingtonville, Ohio 44490. His assembly fits an 8-in. span between the maiden leathers.

If you want to make your own, here are my suggestions: Start with the metal shaft, which is the most difficult. If you have a metal-turning lathe, you're all set. If you don't, you can use a steel rod with copper or steel tubing to form the orifice, and a washer can be soldered or welded in place. The function of the washer is to ride on the inside of the maiden bearing to keep the whole assembly in place. Or, turn the shaft out of wood. The key to making the horseshoe-shaped flyer is accuracy. I cut the outside, then put it on the lathe to make the round section near the orifice and to even up the outside. Before cutting the inside of the horseshoe, I drill the shaft hole while I still have a flat surface on the ends. The flyer, which is permanently attached to the shaft, must be centered and in balance or it will vibrate as it spins. It's going to spin rapidly, because for every pump of the treadle it will rotate from 10 to 20 times, depending on the size of your wheel. Securely pin the flyer to the axle.

The next part is the bobbin. It took me years to realize the bobbin is made in three parts: the shaft, and the two ends. Make the wooden shaft with the wood running lengthwise with the bed of the lathe, and turn the ends of the bobbin with the grain perpendicular to the bed. Drill holes in the ends to receive a glued and force-fit core. The hole in the core must be dead center and true, or again you'll have a wobble. The bobbin has to run free and easy on the shaft—it's never attached. Next make the whorl the same way as the bobbin ends. The whorl is firmly attached to the shaft. The groove in the bobbin for the drive band must be smaller in diameter than the groove in the whorl, so the bobbin will rotate faster than the flyer. This is essential if the wheel is to spin properly. The best way to attach the whorl to the axle is with a lefthand thread on the axle to receive a nut embedded in the whorl. If you don't have the necessary tools, force-fit and pin it. But it is better if the bobbin is removable, so the spinner can remove a full bobbin and replace it with an empty one.

After you know the size of the shaft, cut the maiden bearing leathers and put the holes in them to receive the shaft. A little trick is to use a spade bit in your electric drill. I've always had trouble with leather punches and find drilling more practical. Sole leather for women's shoes makes an excellent bearing material. It should be about ¼ in. thick.

Loose ends and finishes

The drive band is a circle of cord that is folded once upon itself to make a figure eight. The two ends should be spliced or sewn, not tied. The drive band goes around the wheel and around the whorl, and the other loop comes from around the wheel and goes around the bobbin. Before you fit the drive band, screw the tension device so the flyer/bobbin is as near the wheel as possible—even the best drive bands stretch. A

suitable drive-band cord is a small-diameter chalk-line available at most hardware stores. The best is a heavy linen line, braided or plied. A heavy linen fishing line used for trolling is excellent, but hard to find. Spinners usually make their own by plying together about six yarns of thinly spun linen. A linen drive band will last for years, and there's very little stretch. Apply beeswax to the band and put it on.

Decoration is optional: Rope burnings can be done while the leg or upright is still on the lathe, and after sanding, by holding cord (I use chalk-line) against the revolving wood until it just starts to smoke. Or you might carve on the sides of the wheel table, or paint on fancy designs.

Everything should be set to go, except two things. The maiden leathers have to be secured with small wood pins, and the mother-of-all has to be pegged to the upright tension part. Before drilling and doweling, aim the flyer/bobbin pulleys at the wheel. Now, with everything in place, treadle the wheel. A common problem is having the drive-band come off the wheel. There are three remedies: Grasp the wheel supports with both hands and twist to aim the wheel at the bobbin and whorl pulleys; raise or lower the leather bearings in the uprights; or deepen the groove in the wheel. When things are going smoothly, insert pins into the maidens under the mother-of-all, and into the wheel supports under the table. The pins are to keep these members from rotating. Another common problem is having the footman slip down around the pitman arm. The solution is to bend the tip so that it's parallel to the axle shaft.

I usually finish cherry wheels with a good oil-base preparation that will not slow down the wood's natural coloring process. The only problem with boiled linseed oil is that the surface will mildew in hot and humid weather. The old formula of equal parts boiled oil, turpentine, and dark vinegar doesn't seem to mildew as easily. Exposure to sun and air accelerates the darkening of cherry, so I put my completed wheels outside to tan. Tung oil will stop the darkening at any stage you wish. After the finishing is complete, apply a lightweight sewing-machine oil liberally to all places of friction: maiden leathers, wheel-axle leathers, between flyer and bobbin, pitman crank end and treadle-pin holes. Oil regularly, before every spinning. □

AUTHOR'S NOTE: The following firms and individuals sell spinning wheel plans (write them for current prices): Constantine, 2065 Eastchester Road, Bronx, N.Y. 10461 (Colonial flax wheel); Early American Life Magazine, 206 Hanover St., Gettysburg, Pa. 17325 (Saxony wheel); The Woodworkers' Store, 21801 Industrial Blvd., Rogers, Minn. 55374 (Pennsylvania Dutch wool wheel, Colonial wheel, vertical wheel); Woodcraft, 41 Atlantic Ave., Box 4000, Woburn, Mass. 01888 (Welsh sloping wheel, English upright wheel, Norwegian spinning wheel); and Stephan Vannais, 1801 N. Hampton St., Holyoke, Mass. 01040 (Shaker treadle wheel). I've stopped using plans because I've made so many wheels. I work from photographs and from antique wheels in my collection.

The only book I know of about spinning wheels themselves is *American Spinning Wheels* by David Pennington and Michael Taylor, Shaker Press, Sabbathday Lane, Poland Springs, Maine 04274. For information on learning to spin and on spinning accessories, consult *Your Hand Spinning* by Elsie Davenport, Select Books, 5969 Wilbur Ave., Tarzana, Calif. 91536, or *Spinning and Weaving with Wool* by Paul Simmons, Pacific Search Press, 715 Harrison St., Seattle, Wash. 98109.

Bud Kronenberg left advertising copywriting to make and sell spinning wheels in Southbury, Conn.

Five Basic Spindle Laminations

Glued-up turnings produce various patterns

by Ted Pack

Ernest Hemingway used to argue there were only four plots in American novels. If you want to turn out a lamp, rolling pin, inkstand, candlestick or weed pot instead of a novel, your range is increased; I count five basic spindle laminations: the sandwich, the stack, the multiple sandwich, the checkerboard and the chevron.

The sandwich (figure 1) is the easiest lamination. You face-glue a series of boards together, let the glue dry overnight, trim the block and turn. The outer layers follow and accent the piece's curves, making a bull's-eye effect on the front and back; the sides look striped. Making the outer layers thinner than the inner ones will emphasize the bull's-eye effect; making the inner layers thinner emphasizes the striped sides. You can use a range of wood colors, from front to back or from the center slab out, and you can alternate thick slabs of dark wood with thin slabs of light—it's still a sandwich.

Turn a sandwich on its side and you get a stack (figure 2). It's made of short pieces of wood face-glued to one another, with the grain direction alternated for strength. This means your cutting tool will jump from end grain to side grain all along the piece, making this one more difficult to work on. Keep a firm grip and a sharp tool. You can vary the colors and thicknesses of the laminations on this one, too, just like the sandwich. It's a good way to use up ends of boards too short to join and too pretty to throw out.

The multiple sandwich (figure 3) has the bull's-eye effect on all sides, and no striped sides. There are a number of ways to build up the multiple sandwich. I usually turn lamp bases out of them, and so start with a 6-in. by 6-in. core. This can be a solid piece or a glued-up block trimmed square. I laminate to it a thin layer of contrasting wood on each side, then

add a thin layer of the core wood on top of that. This is a good way to use up thin pieces of figured wood. I do not overlap the laminations at the corners, and thus the largest diameter that the finished turning can be is slightly less than the diagonal of the core. This method produces equal-size bull's-eyes on four sides without having to miter the corners of the laminations, which is another way of building up a multiple sandwich. Mitered corners are trickier to cut and glue, but they give you more possibilities for the thickness of the laminations and their proportion to the size of the core. Three, six and eight-sided sandwiches are possible, but the more sides you have, the closer your polygon comes to a circle, and the thinner the laminations will be after turning.

The checkerboard (figure 4) is the most exacting of the five designs shown. To make a block with, say, five strips per side, start with 25 strips that have been planed exactly as wide as they are to be in the final block, and ¼ in. thicker than they are wide. Glue these strips up across the width in an alternating pattern to make five striped boards, two with a dark strip in the center and three with a light strip. When the boards are dry, plane down the extra ¼ in. in thickness, so that each board will be as thick as the strips are wide. Next, glue the five boards into a block, making sure that the ends make a checkerboard pattern. Apply clamping pressure slowly and evenly. I usually put a light clamp at each end of the block and then apply the clamps from the center of the piece out to both ends.

The procedure is the same for any number of squares, but if you pick an even number the center will be in the joint, not the center strip. You can vary the checkerboard design by making the outer layer on all four sides a solid board, the

The Overlapping Multiple Sandwich

Paul Darnell of Phoenix, Ariz., sent us yet another method of gluing up the multiple sandwich, the third of Ted Pack's five basic spindle laminations. Darnell begins with a square core and laminates first only two opposite sides of it. When the glue has dried, he planes the glueline faces and laminates these, overlapping the edges of the first laminations. This process can be repeated until he reaches the limit of his lathe's swing. It produces different-size bull's-eyes on the four "corners" of the turning, as shown in the sample of his work at right. □

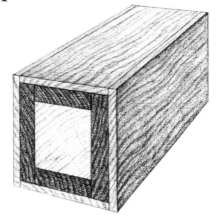

From *Fine Woodworking* magazine (July 1981) 29:52-54

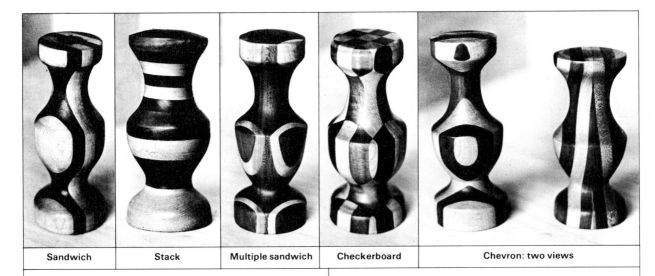

Sandwich	Stack	Multiple sandwich	Checkerboard	Chevron: two views

Fig. 1: Sandwich

Fig. 2: Stack

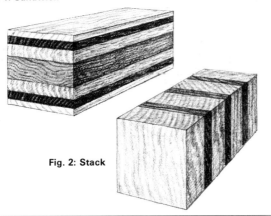

Fig. 3: Multiple sandwich

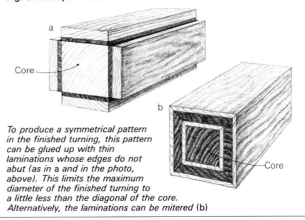

Core

To produce a symmetrical pattern in the finished turning, this pattern can be glued up with thin laminations whose edges do not abut (as in a and in the photo, above). This limits the maximum diameter of the finished turning to a little less than the diagonal of the core. Alternatively, the laminations can be mitered (b)

a

b

Core

Fig. 4: Checkerboard

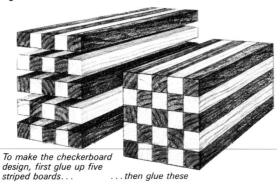

To make the checkerboard design, first glue up five striped boards...

...then glue these into a block.

To vary this pattern enclose the checkerboard with solid boards. This produces accents at the smaller diameters of the finished turning.

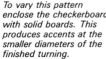

Fig. 5: Chevron

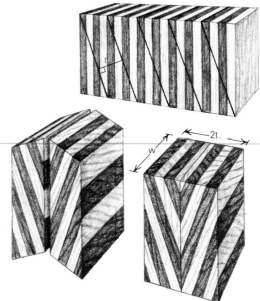

For this pattern, make the angled cut through the slab so it passes through an even number of laminations. Otherwise the contrasting laminations of the half-blocks will not align when reversed and glued up. To produce a square turning block, the thickness (t) of the half-blocks should equal half the width (w) of your laminations.

result being that the interior checkerboard will produce minor accents as it is revealed in turning.

The chevron (figure 5, preceding page) is easier to glue up than the checkerboard, but it takes more time and planning. Face-glue a number of thin slats into a slab, then cut the slab at an angle to make thick slices. Reverse every other slice and glue them into turning blocks two by two. If you've ever made a herringbone cheeseboard you'll recognize the technique.

There are several things to mull over with pencil and paper before you start making noise and sawdust. First, the triangular pieces at the ends are waste, no matter how many turning blocks you get from the middle. For economy, consider making at least two blocks from each slab. Second, to have the light and dark laminations meet in your turning block, you have to cut each half-block so it contains an even number of laminations; the half-blocks in the models and the drawing are four laminations wide.

Look at the sketch again. The true thickness of each half-block will be the altitude of a parallelogram—the line marked t in figure 5. This will be less than the thickness of four slats because of the angle, and the steeper the angle, the more pronounced the difference. The true thickness of two half-blocks should be close to the width of the slats you begin with, to end up with roughly square turning blocks.

After planning your blocks out on a piece of paper, cut the slats and glue up the slab. Let it dry, then plane the top and bottom flat and square with the ends. Now cut the half-blocks, using a bandsaw if possible. Be sure to start and end each cut on a slat of the same color. Plane the sides of each half-block, flip and glue. If you didn't get the bottom quite square, or the bandsaw was a little out of true, the blocks will not match in front and back; at this stage the best you can do is make a perfect chevron in the front and keep the back of the finished piece turned to a wall. Wait for the second application of glue to dry overnight, trim the ends of each block square, and turn.

You can vary the thickness and color of the laminations in this configuration, but you have to do so carefully. If you use very thin slats of maple alternated with thick slats of cherry, for example, you still must have an even number of slats in each half-block. If you use three woods you must maintain the same sequence throughout the slab, and you must have a multiple of three slats in each half-block. The same holds for four, five or more woods.

All of the patterns are easier to do if you have, or have access to, a thickness planer. The checkerboard, in particular, is almost impossible to do without one. If you don't have one, and can't see spending $1,500 to get one, consider signing up for woodshop at your local junior college or night school. School shops usually have a planer, a bandsaw and a lathe. The cost is minimal—I've paid from $3 for an entire semester to $20 for 10 nights—and the teachers do not confine your choice of projects or tool use, once you've demonstrated a reasonable familiarity with basic shop safety.

The best glue joints are produced between freshly planed surfaces and between woods of similar density. Maple, cherry, walnut and koa work well together, as do pine and redwood. I've always thought the pattern, not the wood, was the focus in a laminated turning, so I usually use plain, unfigured wood, and let the lamination speak for itself. □

Ted Pack lives in Riverbank, Calif.

Q & A

Drilling long stock—*I am interested in your experts' methods of drilling a true lengthwise hole in the end of a bedpost or other long piece of stock. Whenever I try to join two long pieces end-to-end, I have great difficulty getting them accurately aligned.*

—*J. Hockenberry, E. Brunswick, N.J.*

CARLYLE LYNCH REPLIES: Here's a way to drill accurate holes in long, turned columns using a drill press.

Turn a hardwood cone with a taper between 60° and 90°, a tenon that fits the center hole of your drill-press table, and a base to keep it from falling through the hole.

On a lathe, center a 1-in. length of ⅜-in. dowel in a 3-jaw chuck, and with a ¹⁄₁₆-in. bit in a Jacobs chuck in the tailstock, drill a hole through the center of the dowel. Turn one end of the dowel to a taper. Thread 3 ft. to 4 ft. of fishing line through the hole in the dowel. Attach one end of the line to a plumb bob, and tie the other end to a washer to prevent that end from slipping through the hole in the dowel.

Chuck the dowel hand-tight in the drill press, making sure that the fishing line isn't trapped between the jaws, but slides freely through the hole in the dowel. Put the cone in the table center hole and lower the table far enough so that the column, drill bit and cone all fit. Lower the plumb bob until it's just above the point of the cone, and clamp the table when you've lined up the points. Remove the dowel, line and plumb bob, and chuck up the drill bit.

Place the tailstock center point in the end of the turned column on the table cone and drill into the spur center point on the other end. Switch ends, putting the hole you just drilled over the cone, and drill into the tailstock center point on the other end of the column. If the column spins while you're drilling, wear a glove or wrap a cloth around it to get a better grip.

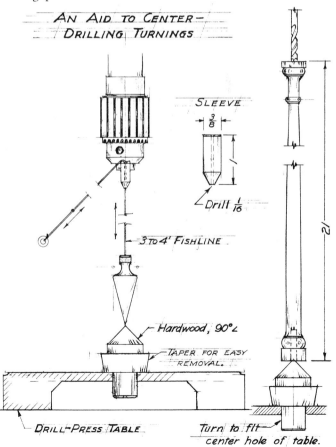

AN AID TO CENTER-DRILLING TURNINGS

SLEEVE

Drill ¹⁄₁₆

3 TO 4' FISHLINE

Hardwood, 90°∠

TAPER FOR EASY REMOVAL.

DRILL-PRESS TABLE

Turn to fit center hole of table.

Turning Thin Spindles
Lacemaker's bobbins demand speed and precision

by Mike Darlow

Turning small yet clean, crisp spindles, such as bobbins for lacemaking, requires a special technique. The professional woodturner who's interested in achieving both speed and quality cannot rely on complicated jigs and lathe attachments because they take time to make and set up and because they limit the range and versatility of his work. But with a simple driving device and a practiced method, ordinary tools can produce the desired results.

Lace bobbins are usually made from fine, straight-grained woods—plum, olive, boxwood and walnut were most commonly used in the past. Bone, ivory and hard softwoods such as yew are also ideal. Being small and slender, lace bobbins require a sound turning technique, particularly with the skew chisel. Though there are varying methods of work, the one I'll describe here is straightforward. Begin by preparing the stock for turning, sawing it into square-sectioned strips whose lengths are determined by the finished length of the bobbin plus an allowance for chucking and parting off.

There are four common methods of holding the wood at the headstock. The traditional way employs a small, pronged driving center. One can be made by turning a piece of hardwood to the appropriate taper and pushing it into the swallow of the headstock spindle. Start the lathe, flush off the projecting end and mark its center with the long point of a skew chisel. Next, stop the lathe, drive a brad into the center and

pinch it off about 6 mm (¼ in.) from the face of the wood. Then with the lathe running, file the brad to a slim point. Now stop the lathe and hammer in two more brads about 3 mm (⅛ in.) from the center pin and diametrically opposite to one another. Pinch them off about 3 mm (⅛ in.) from the face. With this method there is no need to stop the lathe in order to remove the finished bobbin and to center a new blank. To avoid damage to both the skew and the drive center, part off just to the right of the drive center.

The second way uses a steel driving socket on an arbor of appropriate taper. The socket may have either a cone-shaped cavity, with an internal thread to grip the wood, or a pyramidal one. You can easily make the latter from hardwood.

A third way to drive the stock is by means of a jaw chuck. I prefer the Jacobs type because it is small in diameter and has no dangerous projections. This method allows both ends of the bobbin to be finished in the lathe. And because the left-hand end of the stock is held rigidly along the lathe's axis of rotation, the effective diameter of the turning bobbin is increased and there is less chance of breaking it while cutting the long neck. The fourth and simplest method is to push the blank directly into the swallow of the headstock spindle, providing the opening is small enough. Pressure from the ram will keep the wood from slipping while it's being tooled.

Bobbins are usually turned with their heads at the tailstock

What bobbins do

Bedfordshire bobbins work a lace collar. Threads are plaited around pins stuck through holes in the stiff paper pattern into the pillow below.

There are two main types of lace—needlepoint, made by sewing and oversewing with a needle and thread, using mainly buttonhole stitches; and bobbin lace, which uses the weaving and plaiting of threads. It is this latter method of lacemaking that chiefly concerns the woodturner, for he produces much of the necessary equipment, most notably bobbins. Each separate length of thread used in a piece of lace must be wound on a bobbin at each end. Hence, lacemakers refer to a number of bobbins as so many pairs and many prefer to buy their bobbins in identical pairs. A piece of lace can require several hundred pairs of bobbins, but thirty pairs is about average.

Lace bobbins have three distinct functions. First, they store the thread, sometimes up to seven meters in length, and allow it to be fed out as required. Second, they tension the thread. The lacemaker relies upon the weight of the bobbin (and the attached spangles) to provide this tension, and therefore all the bobbins used for a particular piece of lace need to weigh pretty much the same. Third, they weave and plait the threads without soiling them, because

the shank of the bobbin is used as a handle.

There are three main bobbin styles. Continental bobbins follow traditional styles that evolved in particular European lacemaking centers. Honiton bobbins are indigenous to southwestern England. They are used for a fine lace that is usually built up from sprigs—small, complete pieces of lace representing flowers and figures, which are then joined or set into a new ground, using the bobbins as needles. This is why Honiton bobbins have smooth, narrow shanks with pointed ends.

East Midlands Bedfordshire bobbins are slim and basically cylindrical. Most of the bobbin's weight is provided by the spangle. The turner supplies the bobbin drilled, but the spangle is supplied and fixed by the lacemaker. How this unlikely appendage originated is unknown, but spangles—glass beads used as weights—were threaded into 17th and 18th-century laces as decoration. Perhaps a lacemaker wishing to increase the weight of her bobbins tied on some of these spangles, and this evolved into the nine-bead spangle found on East Midlands bobbins from the late 18th century. —*M.D.*

Photos: Henry Strasburger; Illustration: Ric Lopez

end. In the overhand turning method, which is the most common, the left hand either rests on the turning tool or acts as a mobile steady with the left thumb assisting in controlling the tool. The fingers are wrapped over and behind the bobbin to give it support. With this method it's wise to turn the long neck at the tailstock end, as the left hand can more easily support the shank and is clear of the drive center.

I prefer the less common underhand turning method (photo, right) in which the index finger of the left hand goes beneath the tool rest and supports the work, while the thumb and remaining three fingers grip the tool. With this method it's best to turn with the head toward the headstock. This allows the bottom end of the shank to be finished off in the lathe. Finishing off is tricky but can be accomplished by passing the last three fingers of the left hand beneath the bobbin and bracing them against the tool rest, while steadying the right-hand end of the bobbin between the thumb and forefinger. Slacken the tailstock a little to facilitate parting off with the long point of a skew. After withdrawing the tailstock further, you can sand the free end of the bobbin while still supporting it with the thumb and forefinger. Then part off the head. With a little practice you can catch and present the bobbin in your left hand.

Once you've decided on which way to drive the stock, prepare a pin gauge by drawing the bobbin full size on a piece of wood about 13 mm (½ in.) thick. Project main bobbin features onto its edge where you drive in brads that are pinched off to a length of 3/16 in. Then sharpen the brads with a file to screwdriver-like points. When centering your stock, take care not to force the tailstock as the wood may split, and once you've centered it, back off slightly on the ram. Excess axial pressure will cause the spindle to spring into a bow when the long neck is cut.

With the lathe running at its fastest speed, rough out the stock using a shallow-nosed gouge about 19 mm (¾ in.) wide and partially ground off on its left-hand side so that you can rough right up to the headstock. A 7-mm (about 5/16 in.) gouge and a 7-mm skew chisel complete the tool kit. With the lathe still running, lightly press the points of the pin gauge into the rotating wood and then proceed to turn the spindle in the order prescribed in the diagram.

On your first few attempts you may want to caliper the diameters, but it's best to train your eye to gauge them properly. It is preferable to use the skew chisel as much as possible since it's a less risky tool than the gouge. It is possible that the wood will climb up over the nose of the gouge and fracture. When using the gouge, turn it on its side and approach the work obliquely, using it like a skew chisel. The long neck has to be cut with the skew chisel, while either the skew or the gouge may be used to cut the short neck.

I usually sand with 180, then 220-grit aluminum-oxide paper. Traditionally bobbins were not polished, and an attractive patina developed during use. Some turners finish in the lathe, either with beeswax or with a friction polish. I recommend neither, since the wax could soil the thread and the friction polish is slow to apply and too glossy for my taste. After any required hole-drilling, I finish just by dipping in a penetrating oil, which dries completely, brings out the wood colors and leaves an attractive satin sheen. □

Mike Darlow is a professional turner and cabinetmaker in Sydney, Australia.

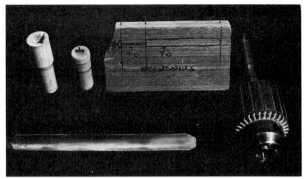

Bobbin turner's tools: wooden driving socket, pronged driving center, pin gauge and Jacobs chuck. Note shape of roughing gouge, ground from a standard spindle gouge.

Turning the long neck using the underhand method. Index finger of left hand reaches below tool rest to support work beneath cutting edge of skew chisel.

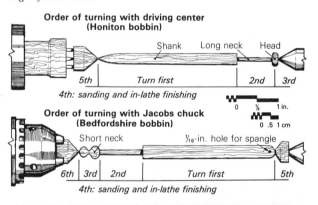

Order of turning with driving center (Honiton bobbin)

Shank Long neck Head

5th Turn first 2nd 3rd

4th: sanding and in-lathe finishing

0   ½   1 in.
0 .5 1 cm

Order of turning with Jacobs chuck (Bedfordshire bobbin)

Short neck 1/16-in. hole for spangle

6th 3rd 2nd Turn first 5th

4th: sanding and in-lathe finishing

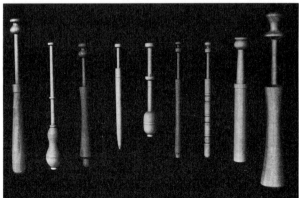

Bobbins, some traditional, some of author's design. The stout ones are for coarse or woolly fibers.

Split Turnings

Using green logs to turn a camel

by John Kelsey

Although it is one of the oldest machines used by man, the lathe is fixed in our minds as a device for making bowls and cylinders. But it is also a multi-purpose machine for making parts of infinite variety — a general-purpose tool whose product is a means to an end rather than an end in itself. If one can visualize a cross-section, one can generate that form in three dimensions by turning. And then one can cut the turning anywhere at all to get an entirely new shape.

Here I will describe the turning of a rocking camel large enough for several children or adults to ride. This project requires a good-sized lathe, a bandsaw or a chainsaw, and hand tools. The materials were a station-wagon load of walnut branches scavenged from an abandoned farm where veneer cutters had removed the boles, one four-foot by five-foot sheet of ¾-inch solid birch plywood and some ¾-inch dowels. The beast was turned from the walnut; the plywood and dowels hold it together.

These methods could be used to make herds of camels or a menagerie of cows, horses, ostriches and giraffes. Indeed, any animal seems possible. But the point is to illustrate an approach to the lathe, using it to turn sculptural parts between spindles. The byproduct is a large toy to delight little children that doesn't cost much money.

I think camels are my favorite animal but I chose one here because my daughter had asked for a two-seater rocking horse. I had access to a large file of photographs of camels in various poses at the local newspaper library. A superb source of animal anatomy is the book *How to Draw Animals* by Jack Hamm (published in paperback by Grosset & Dunlap, New York, 1969; check libraries).

From the photos I blocked out the forms that would be

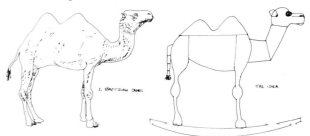

needed. Including the rockers and such details as eyes, ears, tail, the entire camel consists of just ten turned forms; eight or nine could have done it. So much anatomy from so few turnings meant most of them would be cut into two or more parts. This also provides the key to preventing green logs from checking and a way of holding the parts together: fox-wedged dowels pass through a plywood keel or centerboard running from head to tail and dividing the animal in half.

When a log dries it shrinks. Most of the shrinkage is at right angles to the annual rings, or radial, and around the rings, or

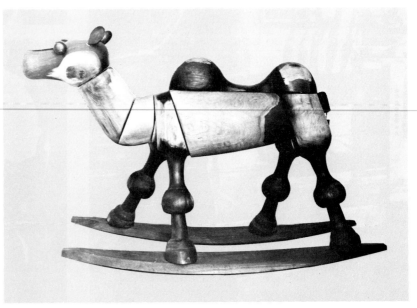

From *Fine Woodworking* magazine (Spring 1976) 2:20-23

tangential. It checks because the circumference is three times as large as the radius — as the rings of wood shrink, they try to squeeze the log smaller and can't. The stresses are relieved by wedge-shaped cracks radiating from the irreducible kernel that is the center of the annual rings. Splitting a log in half before it shrinks allows the stress to be distributed — the cut diameter merely cups as the circumference contracts, and the pieces generally remain intact.

When a tree is felled the exposed end grain dries very quickly and the logs check at the ends. But it takes years for drying to proceed far into a log, and slicing off the end exposes wet, intact material. When such a log is brought into a heated shop and turned, however, the protection of the bark is lost and a large proportion of end grain is exposed. It will check seriously overnight. To avoid trouble, a log should be completely worked in a single day. If it must be left overnight, wrap it in plastic with its own moist shavings, or bury it under a heap of shavings to keep it wet.

Before mangling any camel walnut, I turned a sketchy model at ¼ scale to be sure my conception was reasonable. I worked with photographs near the lathe in an attempt to capture the flavor of flesh in the solid wood. It seems neither reasonable nor desirable to try for realism, and few dimensions will be given here—it is cut-and-try to the scale of the maker's own body.

My largest walnut branch, for the camel's belly and rockers, was 14 inches in diameter including bark, and five feet long. It had a dog-leg crook. I wanted rockers between three and four feet long, so I cut off a chunk to use later for humps and grunted the rest up onto sawhorses. Green walnut weighs about 60 pounds per cubic foot. I use a large, logger's crosscut saw to buck the logs; a chainsaw would have done better and could also replace the bandsaw throughout the job.

I removed the bark with a hatchet and gauged the center by eye, taking into account the crook and aiming to get the largest possible cylinder at the midpoint. Fearing that such a great, uneven mass would not clear the ways of the lathe—a Crescent with a 7½-inch swing radius—and also afraid the log would break free and crush me, I began working it toward round with a power plane and an axe. A conventional center spur quickly tears itself a flat-bottomed hole in soft green stuff, so I use a three-pronged gadget with the usual cup or

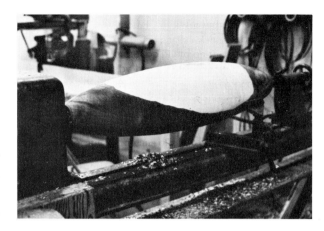

Turned log before it's cut to make belly and rockers

damp this kind of vibration unless one has an enormous lathe such as metal spinners use. Instead, I use a handrest mounted on the lathe ways, not a floor stand, so the hand and tool vibrate in phase with the lathe and log. Obviously, if the tool post fouls the log, one must resort to the floor stand. As soon as the log is cylindrical the vibration mostly ceases, unless the heart and sapwood vary greatly in density and are unevenly distributed through the mass.

Green wood is lovely to turn. I use a one-inch gouge and a large skew, at low speed. The walnut cuts cleanly and quickly —great curly shavings. Fresh surfaces are greenish-brown and turn dark after a few hours' exposure to light and air.

This log was turned to a cigar shape, finishing about twelve inches in diameter at the center and three inches at the ends, and 42 inches long plus an allowance for cutting away the holes left by the lathe centers. The silhouette of this cigar determines the rock of the animal — long and smooth or tight and quick. Any flats left from sloppy turning will be felt as bumps in the ride.

A thin, springy slat can be used as an approximate guide to curvature. I usually sand green turnings to 50-grit, pause for coffee to allow the outer layer of wood to dry a little, and sand to 120 or 150.

The diagram shows how this cigar was cut into four pieces:

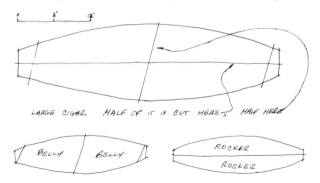

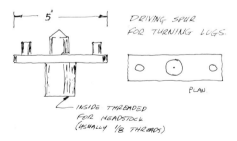

free-spinning tail center. One could also use a faceplate with large screws, but only if the end of the log is cut truly square to the axis of rotation.

I had never turned such a large log before, so I stood well clear when I switched on the machine. The entire lathe bucked and vibrated, but in a steady, rhythmic manner. The log showed no sign of breaking loose. The machine was bolted to the concrete floor, but it was loose on the bolts and this was just as well. If the bolts had been tight, the vibration surely would have cracked its castings. It is futile to try to

two long quarters for the rockers and two crosswise quarters for the belly. The handrest can be used as a pencil guide to lay out the lengthwise cuts before the log comes off the lathe, bearing in mind where the irregular swirl of the yellow sap and brown heartwood will appear in the end. Then I used four plywood squares with circular holes to make a cradle to guide the torpedo slowly through the bandsaw.

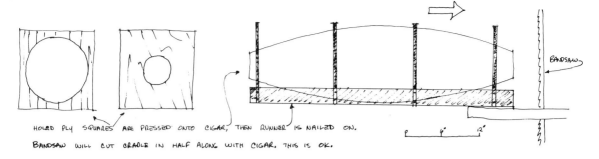

HOLED PLY SQUARES ARE PRESSED ONTO CIGAR, THEN RUNNER IS NAILED ON.
BANDSAW WILL CUT CRADLE IN HALF ALONG WITH CIGAR. THIS IS OK.

The long quarters that form the rockers could be left V-shaped at the top, and the animal's legs mortised to fit. I chose to cut them flat by tilting the bandsaw table to 45 degrees and clamping two small boards to the fence ahead of and behind the blade. This formed a guide trough against

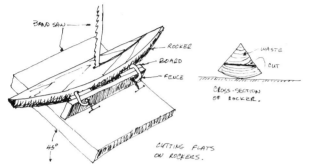

which the curve could run, passing the blade at uniform thickness. (One could make curved staves from turnings for large barrel shapes this way.)

The short quarters that form the belly were bandsawed crosswise, about 15 degrees from square. This angle determines the stride of the camel. The tail ends of these pieces were sawed at a similar angle, so the two sawed faces were approximately parallel, and a flat was planed on top where the humps would go. Most of these faces won't show

Camel is assembled as split turnings are attached to "backbone" of solid birch plywood using dowels and fox wedges.

on the finished beast and needn't be planed smooth. Or else the surfaces can be run over a jointer.

Before making the legs, I bandsawed the plywood to the rough shape of the camel, making sure it was oversize in every dimension, and traced the outline of the belly onto it. Then I drilled three holes for dowels and used the plywood as a template to drill matching holes two inches deep into each half of the belly. The easiest way is to clamp the walnut to the ply and drill through. Later the bottom of each hole would be widened in the direction of the grain for the fox wedges that

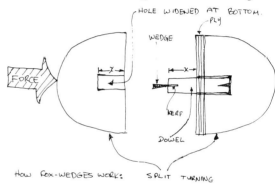

HOW FOX-WEDGES WORK: SPLIT TURNING
FORCE PUSHES WEDGE AGAINST BOTTOM OF HOLE, SPREADING DOWEL & LOCKING IT.

lock the construction together. But for now I used two of the holes to loosely pin the camel's body to the board.

A walnut branch seven inches in diameter and four feet long made a pair of camel legs, joined together at the shoulder. After roughing to a cylinder, I marked a section about a foot long at the center and worked down to a knee and foot at each end, as in the drawing. Then the legs were

TWO LEGS TURNED AS ONE, CUT APART HERE.

cut apart on the diagonal. This flat face butts against the centerboard. To make a clean joint with the belly, and also to loosen up the camel's canter, the front shoulders were cut again on the diagonal to make a second flat face at right

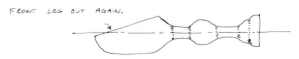

FRONT LEG CUT AGAIN.

angles to the first. The belly is narrow enough at the back to require no second cut on the rear shoulder.

The legs were pinned to each other through the centerboard, just like the body. But because they walk, one dowel from each must go into the opposite belly piece and this strengthens the construction. Although they weren't split in half, the legs haven't checked. I believe this is partly because they aren't very thick and partly because the center of the rings isn't the center of the turnings. Branches grow that way, with more wood on the bottom of a curve than on the top. Thus the center of the annual rings passes through the bulbous foot, knee and shoulder, but is cut away elsewhere. Constructions like this could also be turned with large tenons to fit holes ("circular mortises") like kitchen chairs.

I blocked the camel upright on two sawhorses until the rockers, held level in pieces of the cradle that had guided the large cigar through the bandsaw, could be slipped under the feet. Then, using a small block in the same way that one levels table legs, I marked a base line on each foot and cut them.

A single tapered cylinder made the neck, split in half lengthwise and pieced together to match on each side and form a bend. Dowels hold it together, as usual.

With this much made and loosely assembled, I traced around the walnut and bandsawed the plywood to size — leaving two inches sticking up from the neck to tenon the head on. A little chopping with an in-cannel gouge widened the holes for the wedged dowels. Large clamps forced the beast together. Then I turned the camel over, clamped the rockers into position, drilled through into the feet, countersunk for the heads, and drove six-inch lag screws home.

Saw, Surform and rasp cleaned up the discrepancies between the two sides. When the humps and tail were added, the plywood only showed along the back of the neck. It could have been hidden here too by cutting it undersize and filling the gap with a strip of solid wood.

There must be a million ways to cartoon an animal's head in solid wood. Found, green wood is cheap enough and soft enough to try several variations — on the lathe, you can almost model it like clay. I finally turned a ball with snout, cut a slice off the chin and pinned it back on again to form lips, added a few veiner cuts, and chiseled a deep V-groove for the nose which was one-quarter of a scrap turning. I used a dumbbell-shape for eyes, turned with the center of the rings on center for that spaced-out look, and pinned it into a gouged channel atop the nose. The ears were a small barrel turning with a tenon on each end, cut on the diagonal to make two and driven into holes. I planed the bottom of the

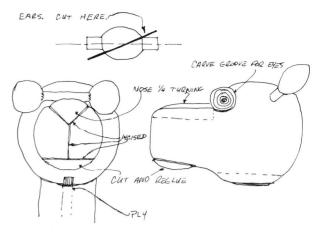

head flat to meet the neck, cut a slot for the ply and fastened it on with two vertical, wedged dowels.

The humps were the most difficult turning to work out. The problem was keeping enough height while paring the width so they would fit atop the body, and retaining a saddle between them. I made a large ball with a thick stem, split it into quarters and removed wedge-shaped pieces as in the

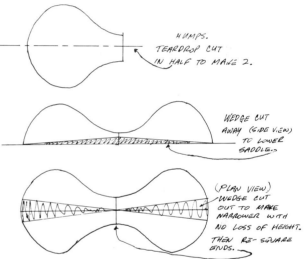

diagrams, and pinned the four parts together. The tail was easy — a cylinder cut in segments and drilled for a length of rope, knotted behind a dowel driven into the plywood. Then sandpaper, several coats of Watco, and a happy child. □

Author Kelsey astride his beast

Coopered Columns

Joining and turning large staved constructions

by John Leeke

Since leaving my father's woodworking shop ten years ago, I have made my living building furniture and cabinets and restoring houses. Occasionally I do rough carpentry for a regular customer, but I would rather stick to finish work. So I was something less than excited when I was asked to repair a porch. My attitude improved quickly when I learned that the house was listed with the National Register of Historic Places. A typical example of a 19th-century mill owner's house, the Goodall House in Sanford, Maine, is a mansard-style mansion with a Colonial Revival porch built in a simple classical style. One of the 9-ft. columns had rotted and needed to be replaced. I hadn't done any lathe work as large as this required, but thought that my small shop just might be able to handle it. Had I known then that in the end I would replace more than a dozen columns, I might not have taken the job.

Now I'm happy I did, for making columns has been profitable for my small enterprise. It took me 38 hours to build the first 9-ft. column. A subsequent run of six columns for the same house required 32 hours per column, and a recent run of six columns for another job took 26 hours for each. These figures include the time I spent developing techniques and making the special jigs and clamps that I'll describe below. The actual production time on the last run of columns was 20 hours apiece. At that rate I can make large columns that are comparable in cost, and at least equal in quality, to those produced by millworks and large manufacturers, even though I use only ordinary, small-shop machinery and tools.

The old columns were 13 in. in diameter and were built up stave-fashion like a wooden bucket. Made of cedar, their lapped tongue-and-groove joints had loosened over the years, even in columns not yet rotted. I decided to join mine with splined miters, and chose resorcinol-formaldehyde exterior glue to keep the joints together. Instead of cedar, I used pine.

Cutting the staves—To begin, I made full-scale drawings of the column in section and elevation (figure 1). The sectional drawing shows the finished diameters of the shaft and the dimensions of the 12 staves. The elevation drawing shows the shaft, plinth, base, bead mold and capital, as well as the curvature of the entasis, the barely perceptible swelling of the shaft towards the middle. In deciding upon 12 staves, I considered the higher cost for fewer staves of thicker stock against the extra labor involved in making more joints with thinner stock. Because a greater number of staves makes the column more stable, I used 12 of them, and as in the original columns, I oriented the annual rings at random.

I cut the rough stock to within 1 in. of finished length, which made it much easier to mount the coopered blank on the lathe. The width of the rough stave blanks was also cut oversize to allow for warping due to relieved stresses in the plank. After jointing one face and one edge on each, I leaned the staves up in a corner of the shop for a few days to allow the stresses to equilibrate. I jointed them again just before cutting the bevel on their edges. The staves must be stable and straight, and should not warp after the bevels are cut, as this would alter the angle of the beveled edge.

For a 12-stave column the bevel is 75°. The accuracy of this cut is important because joints must have uniform contact their entire length. If a cumulative error of 1° is tolerable in the whole ring of staves, then each bevel cut must be within $\frac{1}{24}$ of a degree. To achieve this degree of accuracy I use the compounding-of-the-errors method. To do this, set the tablesaw blade to cut an angle slightly larger than 75° and the fence to cut about $\frac{3}{16}$ in. larger than final width. Then take a set of twelve staves, 10 in. long, and saw one bevel on each. On the first cut leave the blade low enough so the waste remains attached and doesn't get wedged between the blade and the insert (figure 2). Remove the waste by hand and cut the other bevel. Clean the sawdust off of the staves, set them on end on a true flat surface, and butt the edges tightly against one another. Usually a gap of about $\frac{3}{8}$ in. will appear (figure 3). Now reset the sawblade higher and for a slightly smaller angle, and the fence to a slightly narrower width. Pass the staves through the saw again and check as before. Repeat this operation, making minute adjustments in the blade and fence until the gap is closed. Then measure the diameter of the blank across the opposite faces. It should still be somewhat larger than required. With repeated checking and small adjustments to the width of cut, the diameter can be brought to the correct measurement. It usually takes me a couple of hours to get the saw set for this one cut. Once I am satisfied with the setting, I saw the run of staves.

The splines are $\frac{1}{4}$ in. by $\frac{5}{8}$ in. To make sure that the joints would close, I cut the grooves (figure 4) just slightly deeper than needed and wide enough for each spline to be pushed into its slot with my thumb. If the grooves are so narrow that the splines must be tapered or forced into place, final assembly will be very difficult because the glue will swell the splines slightly, making the fit even tighter.

Gluing—I begin by gluing up pairs of staves; then I glue two pairs together to make a third of the column. Finally, I glue the one-third sections together to make the whole shaft. In all the gluing operations I use a clamp every 12 in. when possible and keep the ends of the staves flush to make it easier to mount the shaft on the lathe. When clamping it is best to tighten or loosen each clamp a little at a time.

Gluing up pairs of staves is fairly simple. I made special fixtures with blocks to match the angles of the staves where they meet the clamp jaws. Two sets of clamp heads on each fixture speed handling throughout the production run (photo, top, next page). The one-third sections require clamping pressure from above, as well as from the edges. This is applied by using a frame in which a ½-in. lag bolt is screwed into a hori-

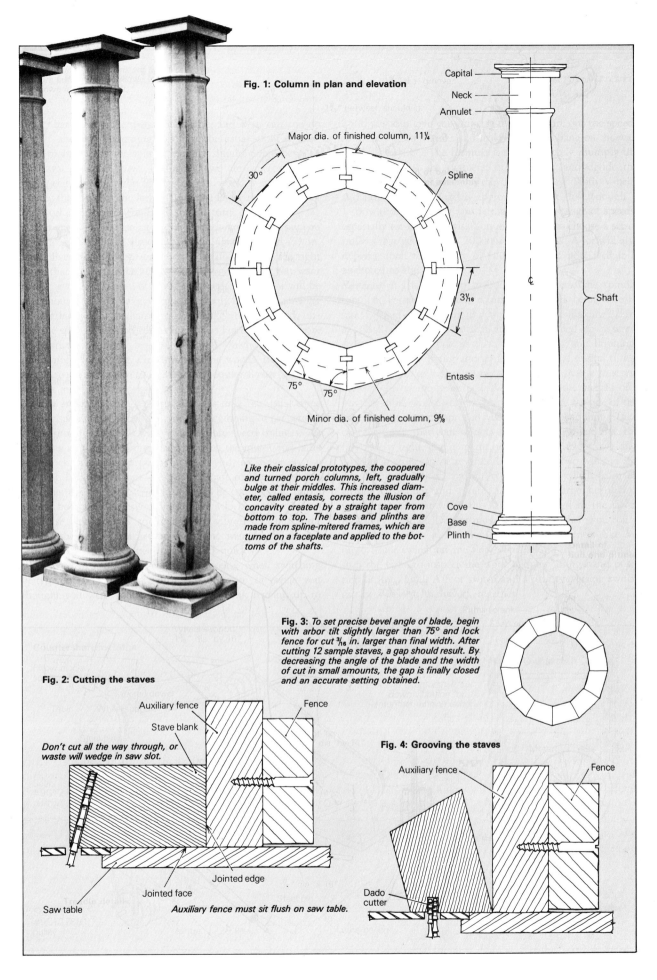

Fig. 1: Column in plan and elevation

Capital

Neck

Annulet

Major dia. of finished column, 11¼

30°

Spline

Shaft

3¹⁄₁₆

75°   75°

Entasis

Minor dia. of finished column, 9⅝

Like their classical prototypes, the coopered and turned porch columns, left, gradually bulge at their middles. This increased diameter, called entasis, corrects the illusion of concavity created by a straight taper from bottom to top. The bases and plinths are made from spline-mitered frames, which are turned on a faceplate and applied to the bottoms of the shafts.

Cove

Base

Plinth

Fig. 3: To set precise bevel angle of blade, begin with arbor tilt slightly larger than 75° and lock fence for cut ³⁄₁₆ in. larger than final width. After cutting 12 sample staves, a gap should result. By decreasing the angle of the blade and the width of cut in small amounts, the gap is finally closed and an accurate setting obtained.

Fig. 2: Cutting the staves

Auxiliary fence

Fence

Stave blank

Don't cut all the way through, or waste will wedge in saw slot.

Fig. 4: Grooving the staves

Auxiliary fence

Fence

Jointed edge

Saw table

Jointed face

Auxiliary fence must sit flush on saw table.

Dado cutter

Pairs of splined staves are glued up using notched blocks and clamping heads (available from Woodcraft, 41 Atlantic Ave., Box 4000, Woburn, Mass. 01888). Using two sets of clamps per bar makes handling easier and gluing faster.

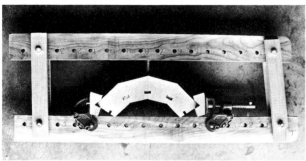

To glue up a one-third section of a column, pressure atop the center joint is applied by a hanger bolt with a knurled face, which is screwed into the top crossmember of a clamping frame. Dry clamping is necessary to get the adjustments right so the joint will close properly when horizontal pressure is applied by the clamps.

zontal clamp bar, which is fastened to the lower clamp bar with ⅜-in. machine bolts and four ½-in. by 2-in. pieces of hardwood (photos, above left and right). The joints of the frame are left somewhat loose so that vertical pressure from the lag bolt can be applied directly over the glue joint. When pairs of glued-up staves are put into the lower clamp bar and the rest of the clamping frame assembled around the staves, the joint is left open at the inside. This gap closes as the screw is tightened and pressure builds up against the lag bolt, flexing the upper horizontal member. If the joint does not have enough pressure when the gap is closed, loosen the clamp and turn the lag bolt down to make the gap bigger. Once each lag bolt is set, it should be correct for the rest of the run. The lag bolt has a knurled pattern filed into it so that it will not slip off the joint. After the clamps are tightened, the width of the section should be checked. Also, check the angle of the two edges with a bevel. If the angle is wrong, more or less pressure can be applied with the clamps to correct it.

After the one-third sections come out of the clamps, the angles should be checked again. Any irregularity along the beveled surface should be corrected with a jointer plane equipped with an adjustable angle fence.

For assembling the thirds into the whole shaft, I first developed a rather clumsy system of forged rings and wedges. This worked well for the first single column, but by the time all of the rings and wedges were set in place and driven up tight I was nearing the end of the glue's closed assembly time. I replaced the forged rings and wedges with clamps made from length of ⅜-in. chain and tightened with 1-in. machine bolts. Each clamp head consists of five parts—a bored steel block through which the bolt passes and to which one end of the chain is welded; a steel nut with a hook machined onto its bottom side so it can grab a link of chain; two steel flanges that are welded to the sides of the bored steel

block; and the 1-in. by 6-in. bolt. Pressure is exerted by tightening the bolt with a wrench, drawing the ends of the chain together. The links will press into the wood quite a bit, but this causes no problem since the outer part of the column is wasted in turning.

On the first couple of shafts, I dry-clamped to make sure everything fit well. Then I spread glue on two joints and set two one-third sections together in semicircular holders. I put glue on the two remaining joints and set the top one-third section on. It took a little jiggling and coaxing with a mallet to get the splines lined up. I placed the heads of the chain clamps on alternate joints around the columns. The semicircular holders made it easy to rotate the columns while clamping.

Setting up the lathe—Few lathes will handle a 9-ft. spindle between centers. To give mine this needed capacity, I hacksawed the ways away from the headstock and mounted the two components the required distance apart on a long, wide bench. You may not want to saw your lathe in half, but if you want to turn long pieces, it's not as destructive an act as you might initially think. The headstock can be bolted firmly in place, the tailstock can still travel back and forth along the detached ways, and the distance between centers is limited only by the size of your shop. It's also quite convenient to have a highly portable headstock for faceplate turning.

I don't particularly like to have large, heavy objects moving at high speeds in my shop. I was concerned about the ability of my lightweight lathe to handle such large stock, so I decided to reduce the rotational speed of my lathe. I made a 22-in. idler pulley out of plywood with a bronze bearing in its center. I glued to the side of it a 4-in. disc, and V-grooved both for belts. The drive belt runs from the motor pulley around the 22-in. pulley; the 4-in. pulley in turn is connected by a belt to the 3-in. mandrel pulley (figure 6, p. 54). This

A jointing plane with metal fence, top left, is useful for correcting any irregularity in the joint interface. Leeke prefers the hand plane over his power jointer for this operation. For gluing and clamping the one-third sections into a full cylinder, Leeke devised and fabricated chain clamps like the one at left from ½-in. chain, steel plate, solid mild steel (for the tapped hook block) and a 1-in. bolt for tightening the chain. The clamp heads are staggered around the column, above, to help equalize the pressure and keep the column's diameter from being squashed into an ellipse.

slowed the lathe down to 100 RPM. I devised a sliding carriage that allowed me to use my router to do the cutting as the stock turned at a slow speed (figure 5, next page). The router (base removed) is equipped with a ½-in. cove-cutting bit and is mounted on a cradle-like block with a 4-in. dia. hose clamp. The cradle is screwed to the plywood carriage. The near end of the carriage is guided by a guide bearing that rides against the edge of a ¼-in. plywood or Masonite pattern board. A rabbeted wooden retainer or metal bracket helps keep the carriage from riding up off the pattern. The far end of the carriage slides underneath an elevated keeper board, which is screwed into the bench top.

Mounting the column—I mounted the columns on the lathe by screwing plates made of ¾-in. hardwood plywood to the ends of each one with 2-in. sheet-metal screws. The screws should pass through the end plate and into the inner one-third of the column wall. These plates have a ⅜-in. hole at the center and were turned and accurately sized to the finished diameter at each end of the column. The column is mounted on the lathe between 60° centers and driven by an angle-iron dog screwed to the plywood head plate, as shown in figure 5 (next page). The dog rides loosely in a slot on the faceplate, which I wrench tightly onto the mandrel as I sometimes use it as a brake during turning to keep the column from rotating too fast. Using this method of driving the shaft, the head plate does not have to be exactly perpendicular to the axis between the centers. In fact, it can be off quite a bit and the column will still turn true because it is held rigidly only between the two 60° centers. This works better than just screwing the faceplate directly to the end plate.

Making the pattern—Specific rules and formulas for developing the proportions and shapes of classical columns can be found in old pattern books, though you may simply reproduce existing columns as I have done. The shaft of the column has a curved outline (entasis), a cove and a fillet at the bottom and an annulet or neck molding near the top. To make the entasis, and to make all the columns in a run the same, a guide template (pattern) is used. To lay out the entasis, mark radius measurements of the finished shape at equal intervals along the pattern perpendicular to a line that is parallel to the axis of the lathe. Connect the ends of these, cut out and smooth the shape with spokeshave and file, and screw the pattern to the bench as shown in figure 5. For long runs, coat the pattern lightly with varnish to preserve the surface, and then wax it.

Turning—Prepare for turning by properly attaching and adjusting the eccentric guide bearing on the sliding carriage. To do this, draw a line on the pattern board that is perpendicular to the axis of the lathe. Now, for optimal cutting angle, slant the sliding carriage at about a 55° angle to the perpendicular, as shown, and bring the router bit into contact with the center of one of the column staves. Clamp the carriage to the pattern board, turn the guide bearing until it contacts the edge of the pattern and then tighten the screw. (Figure 5 shows where to position the guide.) Its eccentric shape will allow you to make fine adjustments in the depth of cut. Now unclamp the carriage, and you're ready to begin turning.

While turning use extreme caution. You have to keep track of two machines, and the exposed router bit is a real hazard. Ear protectors, goggles and a dust mask are essential. I also wear a leather glove to protect my left hand from the downward spray of chips.

Run the lathe for a while to make sure everything is operating correctly before turning on the router. Hold the router assembly firmly against the edge and top of the pattern board

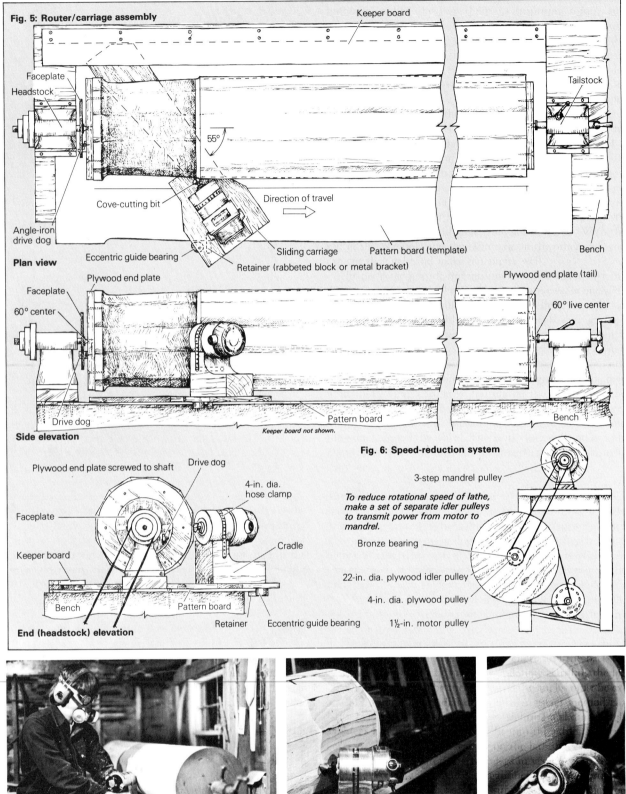

Fig. 5: Router/carriage assembly

Keeper board

Faceplate

Headstock

55°

Tailstock

Cove-cutting bit

Direction of travel

Angle-iron drive dog

Eccentric guide bearing

Sliding carriage

Pattern board (template)

Bench

Plan view

Retainer (rabbeted block or metal bracket)

Plywood end plate

Plywood end plate (tail)

Faceplate

60° center

60° live center

Drive dog

Pattern board

Bench

Side elevation

Keeper board not shown.

Plywood end plate screwed to shaft

Drive dog

4-in. dia. hose clamp

Fig. 6: Speed-reduction system

3-step mandrel pulley

To reduce rotational speed of lathe, make a set of separate idler pulleys to transmit power from motor to mandrel.

Faceplate

Bronze bearing

Keeper board

Cradle

22-in. dia. plywood idler pulley

Bench

Pattern board

4-in. dia. plywood pulley

Retainer

Eccentric guide bearing

1½-in. motor pulley

End (headstock) elevation

Routing from headstock to tailstock, with the router carriage canted at 55°, causes the cove-cutting bit to push itself away from the cut instead of digging into it. At left and center, the staved shaft is being roughed into round in a single light pass. At right, the completed shaft is sanded using a belt sander turned upside down and slid along the column as it turns.

Fig. 7: Cutting the base

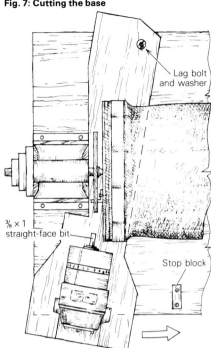

Lag bolt and washer

³⁄₈ × 1 straight-face bit

Stop block

To produce a perfectly flat, perpendicular bottom, the router carriage is bolted to the bench at its far end, and the router is pivoted into the work (drawing, left), cutting through the base plate into the shaft. The carriage is clamped into position and the column is rotated by hand. The straight-face bit is set to cut one-third of the way through the column wall (photo, below), and the cut is finished with a handsaw, which is guided by the inside wall of the groove.

Fig. 8: Plinth and base
Leave square for making plinth. For making base, bandsaw a rough circle, mount on faceplate, turn round and turn molding.

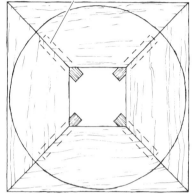

Spline   Molding profiles

with the left hand. Then turn the router on and position the right hand as shown in the photo, facing page, far left. With the guide pressed against the edge of the pattern, start from the left end, and round off the entire shaft in one pass. The cut should be made by sliding the carriage slowly towards the tailstock. When the router bit is cutting on the right side of its center axis and the router assembly is moving towards the tailstock, the bit tends to push itself out of the cut, instead of digging in, and is easier to control. Avoid sliding the carriage from right to left, because this could damage the workpiece or cause injury.

Once the column is cylindrical, you're ready to turn it to its finished diameters. Adjust the eccentric guide bearing for a deeper cut, and begin to waste the bulk of the wood with short cuts, beginning about 10 in. from the tailstock and routing to the right. Then move to the left 10 in. from the beginning of the previous cut and rout again to the right. Continue along the entire column, roughing it to within ¹⁄₁₆ in. of its finished diameter. The final cut is made in one long, uninterrupted pass from left to right, having made a last adjustment in the eccentric guide bearing.

The column's neck and base moldings are not featured on the pattern. I marked out their positions and leave unwasted stock for them when making the rough and final cuts. Then I clamp a tool rest to the bench atop the pattern board and form the moldings with scraping tools sharpened to a rough-ground edge.

The router bit leaves a rough surface that must be sanded. I use a belt sander, sliding it upside down along the top of the pattern board, with the sanding belt working against the column as it turns. Making one pass with a 40-grit belt and another with an 80-grit belt will leave a surface that is good for painting.

In order for the column to stand up straight, the bottom must be cut so that it is exactly perpendicular to the axis of the shaft. Make this cut with a ³⁄₈-in. by 1-in. straight-face bit

in the router. The depth of cut should be set to one-third the thickness of the column wall. Bolt the far end of the sliding carriage to the bench top, and clamp a stop block to the pattern board as shown in figure 7. Use the indexing pin of the headstock to lock the column in position. Holding the carriage down firmly on the pattern board, pivot the router toward the column, cutting through the plywood end plate and into the base of the shaft. When the carriage contacts the stop block, switch off the router, and clamp the carriage to the pattern board. Switch the router back on, release the indexing pin and slowly rotate the column by hand. This will produce a very accurate cut around the base of the shaft. Turn the column away from you while cutting, or the faceplate may unscrew. Take the column off the lathe and remove the plywood end plate. Using the inside wall of the groove for a guide, cut off the waste on the end with a handsaw.

Bases—I make the separate round bases and square plinths with splined-miter joints (figure 8). I make the bases by first roughing them into shape on the bandsaw and then truing them up on a faceplate, after which I turn the various molding profiles with scraping tools. On one run of columns, I needed extra-wide stock on the bottom for a cove molding. I trued the bottom of the columns before turning them and fastened on a 1½-in. thick base with screws and sealed it with butyl caulk, which allows the column to expand and contract.

To increase efficiency in the future and to expand the range of my work, I plan to develop an automatic travel for the sliding router carriage and a system for gluing up all the staves at once, instead of having to glue up each blank piecemeal. I am also working on a method for making tapered and bent-stave columns and on plans for a large router fixture that will let me produce fluted columns. □

John Leeke, assisted by his son Jon (see pp. 82-83), works wood in Sanford, Maine.

Tips From a Turner
Make your own mini drive centers

by Allan Turner Hedstrand

Ready-made spur centers are oversized, clumsy things if you're turning small work. In the mid-1970s, when I was turning miniature spinning wheels and vases, I devised some mini-centers that don't get in the way. These are made from steel rod and are fitted into a Jacobs chuck at the headstock.

A standard spur center has a center point and four sharp prongs that grip the work. The center point has one main function: if you punch a centerhole into the

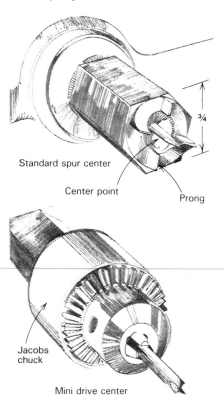

Standard spur center

Center point

Prong

3/4

Jacobs chuck

Mini drive center

end of a blank, the center point will slide into that hole as you snug up the tailstock and will keep the work centered until the drive prongs seat themselves. Some people think that the center point keeps the blank securely on the lathe as well, a little

insurance against the blank flying off and hitting someone. Well, I suppose this is true if you are a heavy-handed turner whose tactics force the prongs to tear loose from time to time. But with miniature work, such insurance isn't necessary. In the first place, cuts are light, and no decent turner is likely to tear the prongs loose. In the second place, the workpiece itself is so light that even if you do knock it off, it won't hurt you. The point of all this, if you will pardon one mild pun, is that you don't really need a point. It's optional.

I made my mini-centers from steel-rod scraps that I had around at the time. These happened to be 3/16-in., 1/4-in. and 1/2-in. diameters. The larger two have no center points. To make a center without a point, cut off a piece of rod about 1¾ in. long and file four cutting prongs as shown in the drawing below. The file alone works fine for the 3/16-in.

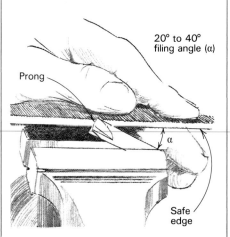

Prong

20° to 40° filing angle (α)

α

Safe edge

rod, but for the larger sizes you can speed the job by hacksawing most of the shape.

If you do want a center point, make it before you file the prongs. Chuck the rod at the headstock and drill a centerhole in the end. A 1/16-in. bit is large enough for rod sizes smaller than 3/8 in. Don't bother setting up the bit in a chuck in the tail-

stock—fit it in a spare chuck and hand-hold it while the rod turns. Next drive a nail into the centerhole until it's tight and you can't pull it out. If you don't have the right-size nail, fit an oversized one in the chuck on the lathe and turn the nail down with a file or a whetstone. If the nail is slightly loose in the centerhole, prick-punch around the hole to tighten it. Then clip it off so it protrudes about 1/8 in.

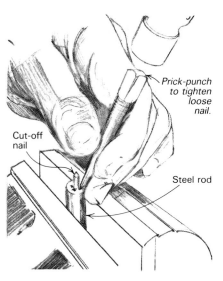

Prick-punch to tighten loose nail.

Cut-off nail

Steel rod

With the rod turning in the lathe, file or stone the center point until it runs dead true. If you're using a file, make sure it has a safe edge so you don't wear away the end of the steel rod. Then file the prongs, being careful not to mar the point. As a final touch, I mark one of the prongs with a small nick, as an aid in repositioning work that has to be returned to the lathe.

When mounting work, I usually saw two cuts into the end of the blank to seat the prongs, and if I'm using a drive center with a point, I poke a hole with an awl. This extends the life of the center. Mine, even though they're made of mild steel, have lasted a long time.

Drawings: Bruce Bulger

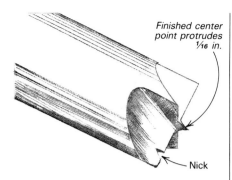

Finished center
point protrudes
¹⁄₁₆ in.

Nick

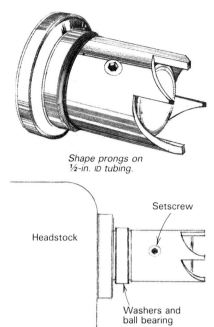

Shape prongs on
¹⁄₂-in. ID tubing.

Headstock

Setscrew

Washers and
ball bearing

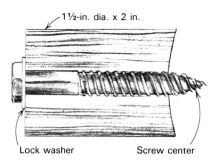

1½-in. dia. x 2 in.

Lock washer   Screw center

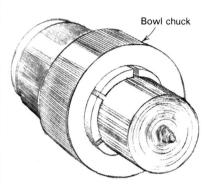

Bowl chuck

Frank Pain, in his book *The Practical Wood Turner* (Sterling Publishing Co., 1979), says that the production turners in his day had a two-prong spur center (which he calls a fork center). This design would be even easier to make than the four-prong design, but if you want to try one, be sure to include a center point. It's easy for these wedges to slide off center otherwise. And, as Pain points out, file a dead spot on each prong near the center, so the shape doesn't wedge itself too deeply into the work.

Another drive center that has proved useful in my shop fits over a ½-in. dia. mandrel on a wooden lathe I once made (altogether I've made six or seven). It's simply a ½-in. ID steel tube with four

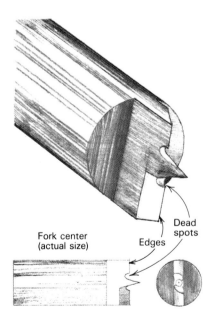

Fork center
(actual size)

Edges

Dead
spots

prongs filed as shown. I drilled and tapped a hole for a setscrew to keep it in place, and slid two washers and a ball-bearing race over the mandrel to take the pressure against the tailstock. I've used this hollow center a lot because it grips well without penetrating deeply, so it minimizes waste when I'm turning tiny vases. Originally, I fitted it with a center point by drilling directly into the end of

the mandrel and banging in a ⅛-in. dia. steel pin. But I've never found the center point to be necessary.

For regular-size bowls, I bought a lathe chuck designed to grip a 1½-in. foot on a half-turned bowl so that you can turn the inside without having to screw a faceplate to the bottom. Many chucks operate on similar principles—they either grip a projecting foot or extend to lock into a depression. In theory, you turn the outside of the bowl (and the foot) while the blank is mounted on a faceplate or a screw center, then remove the bowl, fit the chuck to the bowl and to the lathe, and turn the inside. Well, I didn't like the idea of all that faceplate-and-chuck changing, and I devised a screw center to fit the chuck, so that I could do the whole job without ever removing the chuck from the lathe.

To make the screw center, I turned a piece of prickly-ash branch to a 1½-in. diameter and bored a ³⁄₁₆-in. centerhole clear through. Reversing the blank in the chuck, I enlarged the hole to ¼ in. partway to accept a lag-screw shank. With this size hole the wood grips the shank so tightly that usually I can center a bowl blank on the lag screw without even removing the screw chuck from the lathe chuck. A lock washer adds some extra resistance to turning. If the lag screw does turn when I'm screwing on a blank, I simply remove the screw center from the lathe chuck and hold the bolt head with a wrench while I screw the blank. But this seldom happens, not even when I've backed out the lag screw a little to prevent it from

going too deeply into thinner stock.

Of course, there are times when you want to reverse and recenter the work on a single faceplate. Here's another trick: Screw the blank to the faceplate and turn the outside of the bowl as usual, flattening what will be the foot. Without removing the blank from the lathe, glue scrapwood to the foot (with paper in the joint so you can split off the wood later) and bring up the tailstock to clamp things until the glue dries. Then recess the face of the scrapwood to the exact diameter of your faceplate. When you screw the faceplate into the recess, it will be exactly centered. This takes for granted that your faceplate runs true. If it doesn't, it's easy enough to true it with a file as it turns.

Here's one last tip that might help you someday. I once combined two lathes, because one had a fine bed and the other had a decent headstock. In the process, I went from a Morse taper #1 to a Morse taper #2, which meant that one of my old drive centers no longer fit. I made an adapter from seasoned persimmon wood by turning it to a taper—testing with chalk as I went along—until it didn't wiggle in the #2 taper swallow. I tapped it into place, then bored a hole in it and tapered that to accept the #1 taper on the old drive center. The adapter still runs perfectly true and doesn't slip, even after four years. □

Allan Hedstrand, a self-taught turner, lives in Brooksville, Fla.

Olivewood goblet (left) is 9 inches high. Olivewood bowl is 10 inches in diameter. 12-inch chalice (below) is of kingwood.

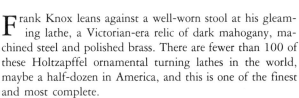

Ornamental Turning

An intricate and exacting pastime

by John Kelsey

Frank Knox leans against a well-worn stool at his gleaming lathe, a Victorian-era relic of dark mahogany, machined steel and polished brass. There are fewer than 100 of these Holtzapffel ornamental turning lathes in the world, maybe a half-dozen in America, and this is one of the finest and most complete.

Mounted between centers is a solid vase-shape of hard, East Indian rosewood, perhaps eight inches long and two in diameter. The lathe has a foot treadle underneath and great, grooved drive wheels but these are disconnected. Electric motors will do the work.

Knox selects a tiny, polished cutting bit from among several hundred precisely arranged tools he keeps in a wooden chest that John Jacob Holtzapffel himself made, 125 years ago. The lathe has an intricate compound slide rest, like the ones metalturners use. This carries the cutting frame, a tool post with a chuck for the little fly cutter, and pulleys that will whirl it around in a high-speed circle. This particular frame, the vertical cutting frame, whirls the bit like a single-toothed circular saw: vertical, with its axis parallel to the axis of the lathe itself.

He makes a number of adjustments and sets some stops but does not turn on the lathe itself; the work remains stationary. The whirling tool slides in, snicks a little facet in the side of the vase, and slides out again. Knox rotates the work a few

degrees and snicks off another tiny facet just touching the first. Soon there are 16 facets making a band, perhaps a tenth of an inch wide, all around the vase.

Should he choose to decorate the entire surface of the vase in this manner, he will have to make a thousand or more little cuts. Knox would be here all afternoon, winding the cutter in and out, counting the holes in the index plate that rotates the work.

If he puts the pin in the wrong hole just once, the piece will not be perfect. If he catches the error right away he will be able to fudge it. Or else he will have to start over, making the whole vase just a little smaller, counting the holes, setting the pin and winding the cutter in and out.

This is complex and ornamental turnery, an intricate and most exacting method of turning forms with more than one axis of revolution, and of decorating the surface of turned forms. In its heyday it was the hobby of kings, princes and the very wealthy. Nobody else could afford the machine, the ivory that is considered the best material, or the time.

Knox is a semi-retired management consultant who, at 70, can afford to be aristocratic in his tastes and his manner. He is an authority on the design of business forms, on controlling paperwork in a bureaucracy, and on integrated cost control. He's written a couple of books about it. He likes precision and order. There is a similarity between gaining an overview

From *Fine Woodworking* magazine (Fall 1976) 4:46-49

Knox's Holtzapffel lathe, made in 1853, has machined iron ways mounted on mahogany uprights and feet. Overhead arm carries pulley drive for cutting frame; weighted pivot arrangement maintains power as sliderest moves. Wooden pulley and treadle, originally connected to brass headstock pulleys, required leg thrust of 45 pounds and is replaced by two motors, one not shown for lathe itself and one on arm for cutters. At right, horizontal cutting frame is mounted on compound slide rest, which is set parallel to ways for between-center turning. Cords and pulleys bring power from overhead motor. Tiny cutter at center of vertical shaft would cut reeding about 1/5-in. wide. Slide rest mainscrew has 10 threads to an inch and crank is calibrated to 1/200-in. Stops can be set to control horizontal and cross feed; shaped handle atop tool box propels cutter to workpiece and out again.

of business paperwork and keeping track of all those little facets.

The earliest ornamental turning lathes were made around 1700 and consisted mainly of thread-cutting lathes with devices for holding the work off-center. The independently driven cutting frame—the basis of the art today—was introduced around 1800, and no lathes were made after 1900.

The machine was perfected during the 19th century by the Holtzapffel family, toolmakers in London, who also compiled a five-volume treatise titled *Turning and Mechanical Manipulation*. The fifth volume is back in print, by Dover Publications, and is devoted exclusively to complex and ornamental turning.

Most of the lathes that still exist belong to members of the Society of Ornamental Turners. This group thought it knew the whereabouts or ultimate fate of every Holtzapffel machine until 12 years ago when its secretary, Wilfred Osborne, turned up a beautiful, disused specimen in an English schoolteacher's attic. Osborne got it for what Knox admits was a song and shipped it overseas with this advice: "Retire, and teach your wife to sharpen tools."

The machine arrived at Knox's midtown Manhattan apartment in a single 3,600-pound crate, and had to be unpacked on the truck to be toted inside. The next few years were spent with Holtzapffel's cryptic book, figuring out some of the things it could do. Knox keeps the machine, along with his Shopsmith and hundreds of blocks of rare hardwoods, in a room down the hall from his elegant apartment.

The key to the lathe is its division plate, a heavy brass disc that is part of the headstock. It has four circles of tiny holes drilled in its face: 360 holes in the outermost ring, then 144, 120 and 96. A little arm with a pin catches the holes, allowing the work to be rotated in increments as fine as a degree and locking it in place. To make a round turning into a 24-sided polygon, one would use the 96-hole circle and put the pin into every fourth hole. For 16 facets, use every sixth hole. Recall that the end of the cutter is perhaps 1/10-inch wide. When the first band has been cut right around the vase, Knox can use, instead of the first and fourth hole, the second and fifth. The stacked 24-gons will then be one hole out of phase, and so will step their way around the form. When the entire smooth surface has been turned into tiny, precise facets, the vase will appear to twist in a spiral.

Of course, Knox is not likely to wreck a pretty little vase by cutting a thousand facets on it. But he has been known to use an even smaller bit to put that many minute facets on the stem of a drinking goblet, or on a candleholder, or a peppermill. When the cutter is very small the facets disappear, creating a strange, knurled texture superimposed on the grain of the wood that the eye can't quite resolve but the hand can feel.

It is not possible to sand this kind of work, and so a razor-sharp cutter is essential. So too is a material that will not tear. Ivory is said to be the best but it is too expensive to consider these days. Blackwood is good, although large pieces are often flawed and must be patched with epoxy. Many of the tropical

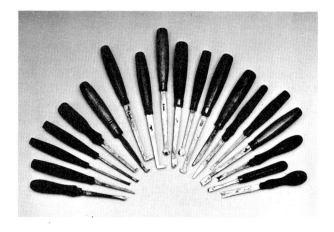

These are the cutting frames which mount on the compound slide rest and carry the tools. They are driven by an overhead belt. The difference between them is the orientation of the whirling or revolving tool. The top left is the universal cutting frame, which has a pivot at its elbow and may be set at almost any orientation. Top right is the horizontal frame; a reeding cutter is visible on the vertical shaft below the single pulley. At center left is the vertical cutting frame—the tool fits into the slot at the end of the shaft and whirls parallel to the pulley. This is the frame Knox uses to cut a 24-gon band around a vase. Center, the eccentric cutting frame, which allows the bit to describe circles of varying sizes on a moveable axis. Center right is an original drilling frame, and at bottom is a modern drilling frame with a conventional Jacobs chuck. Photo at right shows some plain turning tools that came with the Holtzapffel.

hardwoods work well, particularly lignum, snakewood, cocobolo, rosewood, kingwood, camwood and amaranth.

The Holtzapffel tool box contains perhaps 400 cutters. Knox says he uses a dozen for most of his work, half of the rest once in a while, and the other half he hasn't ever used.

The lathe operates in three basic modes: (1) the work revolves with the tool stationary, as in ordinary turning; (2) the work is stationary and the tool is on the fly, like a milling machine; and (3) both the work and tool move in concert, as in cutting threads.

The various cutting frames orient the axis of the circle described by the whirling tool: parallel to the axis of the lathe, at right angles to it, or at an angle in between. Some of the tools are made to revolve like a drill and fit a standard chuck, although their tips may be shaped to cut pearls or stepped holes. The work itself, whether between centers or on a faceplate, can rotate on center, or off-center in a precisely controlled way, or it can be made to describe an ellipse rather than a circle. There is even a dome chuck on which to mount the work vertically, for cutting flutes on a hemisphere.

One begins to see some of the possibilities of such a machine. Consider a small bit with a semicircular notch cut in its end. Set in the horizontal cutting frame and allowed to traverse a straight-sided cylinder, it would cut nice, clean reeding. The machine comes with 16 brass gears that can be used in various combinations to connect the slide rest to the spindle itself, thereby cutting spirals ranging from 40 turns to an inch up to one turn in seven inches. Now the nice, clean reeds wind around the cylinder. Finally substitute a curvy vase for the cylinder, and make a template the shape of the vase. The slide rest will follow the template, and the reeds will wind their way around the curvy vase.

A similar bit with a round shank, chucked in a drilling frame, would make a little hemisphere, a half-buried pearl. Put them in a ring about the base of a chalice, or along it in a row. The toolbox contains bits for pearls of all sizes, and for their corresponding dimples. Some of the bits are stepped, to cut a stack of tiny discs of decreasing size, or inversely, a round, stair-stepped pit. Some cut a full reed or flute. Others cut half of a reed and half of the reed adjacent. Sharpening is a major chore and the toolbox contains two goniostats for holding the bits on the stone at the proper angle, one for flat cutters and the other for curved. Concave curves are honed on a series of little brass cones, spinning on a shaft and charged with abrasive powders.

An exercise in Holtzapffel's book is a series of what appear to be ivory spirals. In fact, each amounts to a stack of discs, the center of each disc offset slightly from the ones above and below. When the ivory is center-bored before turning the discs that form the spiral, and the hole plugged with a core of wood that is later removed, the result is an intricate ivory spring. The "celestial spheres" originally hand-carved in the Orient—an ivory sphere within a sphere within a sphere—were occasionally made by Victorian ornamental turners to demonstrate the capabilities of their lathes. The Science Museum in London has a square Gothic church tower made by Holtzapffel in ivory, 21 inches high, that appears to be a replica of Chartres or Westminster, complete with classical arched windows, delicate tracery and all the ornate trimmings. It was made entirely on the lathe.

Of all the strange attachments devised for ornamental lathes, the wierdest must be the geometric chuck. Originally developed in France as an instrument for drawing the curves arising from the planetary motions of two circles, it was adapted to the lathe about the middle of the 18th century. One end of the device screws onto the lathe spindle and the other carries a duplicate spindle, on which to mount the work, usually a flat plate or disc. Modern plastics work quite well. The two spindles are connected by an intricate arrangement of planetary gearing. The workpiece may be set off-center and geared to rotate either faster or slower than the spindle. Thus a stationary tool will inscribe an epicycloidal curve on the work, rather like the curve made by a child's Spirograph toy. Such a device may be made in more than one stage, as if several were mounted one atop the other. The resulting curves are fantastically interlooped rosettes. Holtzapffel made three of these geometric chucks with four stages, and one with seven stages. Even with the simplest of settings,

Above, a drilling frame holds a cutter that is making pearls on a vase surface. At right, a vertical cutting frame holds a straight cutter that is making tiny facets of polygonal bands about the East Indian rosewood vase shape. Below, Knox holds an example of spiral turning, while bottom photo shows eccentric chuck. This substitutes a spindle that can be set off-center for the lathe's own spindle. The chuck holding the work screws onto the eccentric nose. Now the entire chuck and the off-center workpiece can rotate on the axis of the lathe, or the work alone can rotate on the axis of the eccentric nose. In the background is the division plate with its rows of holes. The arm at left carries a pin to index the holes. The screw atop the arm allows for fine adjustment.

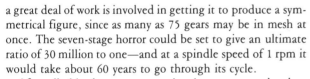

a great deal of work is involved in getting it to produce a symmetrical figure, since as many as 75 gears may be in mesh at once. The seven-stage horror could be set to give an ultimate ratio of 30 million to one—and at a spindle speed of 1 rpm it would take about 60 years to go through its cycle.

After all this the proper question is, can a woodworker dabble here by modifying his own machinery? Knox doesn't think so. But Tubal Cain, writing several years ago in the British magazine *Woodworker*, suggests otherwise.

A metal-working lathe is more appropriate than a woodworking lathe because it already has a compound slide rest, a more suitable speed range, and is more rigid. Cain suggests first adding a division plate with which to index the work, recommending rings of 144, 120 and 96 holes. The 360-hole ring is too fine to be of much use.

A drilling frame to fit the tool post could be made by end-drilling a bar of the appropriate size and inserting a shaft with bearings and a pulley on one end and a Jacobs chuck on the other. It could be driven by a separate motor and small belt, or by a flexible shaft and router or Dremel.

A cutting frame would require more difficult machining, but Cain supplies a drawing. The key things are good bearings and absolutely no slop. Cutters should be made of silver steel, tempered to straw, and from 1/4 and 3/16-in. drill rod.

The most-used special chuck is the eccentric chuck. One could contrive to attach a lathe topslide to a faceplate, providing there is enought clearance over the ways.

In the 12 years since he acquired his obsession, Knox has completed 102 objects. Some contain as many as 13 different pieces of wood. He says some of his 275 fellows in the Society of Ornamental Turners are fascinated by the intricacy of the machine, while others, like himself, enjoy doing the work and the final result.

''I look at myself only as an instrument for bringing out the beauty of the wood,'' he says. ''The surface decoration must be complimentary to the wood—one hopes the applied decoration enhances the wood itself. You have to be clear about what you are going to do when you start, but often you don't end up with what you thought. The machine has its limitations, but nobody has yet explored those limitations and probably nobody ever will.'' □

Holtzapffel Revised
A modern ornamental lathe

by Roger Holmes

Two hundred years ago John Jacob Holtzapffel, a German immigrant to England, built an extraordinary lathe for ornamental turning. Part wood lathe, part machinists' lathe, part router jig, this bewilderingly complex device was used commercially for security printing (to inscribe intricate patterns on plates for bank notes, for example) as well as for the elaborate decoration of items turned of ivory and some exotic woods by amateur enthusiasts. *Wealthy* amateur enthusiasts: in 1838 one of the more complex models cost as much as several houses.

About seven years ago Ray Lawler got bitten by the ornamental turning bug. He soon discovered that ornamental lathes were as pricey as they were scarce: only some 350 of the 3500 or so lathes made between 1795 and 1914 by Holtzapffel, his descendants and his imitators survive. So Lawler and his father, Calvin, decided to build their own in the machine shop of their Kansas City, Mo., gear company. Figuring there must be other would-be ornamental turners out there, they designed the machine for production in small batches. The Lawlers expect to have enough orders to make the first run of 20 machines, selling for about $8,000 each, sometime during the winter of 1985/86.

I saw the prototype in May 1985 in Kansas City; it's a beautiful machine. The warm glow of cast brass, the dull luster of precisely machined steel, the black enameled frame and massive mahogany legs evoke the machine's 19th-century ancestors. But the Lawler (as I suspect it will become known) is more than an ele-

gant copy. For starters, it's much bigger than most of the originals: a hefty lead screw spans the full 36 in. between centers as opposed to Holtzapffel's 12-in. screw and 24-in. centers; the Lawler swings 14 in. over the bed, the Holtzapffel only 10 in. The Lawler also has a redesigned slide rest, cutting frames and pulley system, spiraling gears and other features to make it easier to set up and operate than the originals.

The Lawler benefits from technology unknown to the 19th century. The electric motor is obvious, less so are the linear ball bushings supporting the slide rest on round steel ways, which deflect only .005 in. under 250 lb. pressure. Nonetheless, Ray Lawler has a healthy respect for the machinists who handmade the old lathes. He figures it took one man several weeks to accurately bore the 800-plus indexing holes in the headstock pulley. With about two hours of programming and setup, Lawler's computer-controlled mill does the same job in 18 minutes.

From screws to complicated fixtures, every part of the old machines fits one machine only; replacements had to be made, not bought. Lawler used as many stock parts as possible, so that if something needs fixing, you can buy it off your local machinery supplier's shelf. The machine also conforms to the critical gearing, threading and indexing specifications of the Holzapffel machines. As a result, Holtzapffel's exhaustive treatises on ornamental turning will be Lawler's operator's manuals. And for ordinary turning, the spindles accept standard Delta lathe accessories.

Ray Lawler did much of the design work on the lathe from pictures in books, but he's quick to spread the credit. He's consulted frequently with ornamental turners Frank Knox, Walter Balliet and Daniel Brush. Knox, a long-time enthusiast, has done a great deal to make ornamental turning known outside the tiny circle of lathe owners (see pp. 58-61). Balliet, a retired tool-and-die maker, built his own machine, and Brush owns one of the most complete Holtzapffels in the world. An eager and talented staff at Lawler Gear wrestled with various technical problems, and all are anxious to help work bugs out in several months' field testing before the first production run.

Because the old lathes are so scarce, it's difficult to estimate demand for the new ones, but being the only producers of ornamental lathes in the world is a healthy market position. Sales, though, seem to be icing on the cake for the Lawlers. "If we don't even sell a single machine," Ray told me, "we've had a lot of fun researching it. And we've got one to play with ourselves." □

Roger Holmes is an associate editor of Fine Woodworking. *For more information contact Lawler Gear Corp., 10220 E. 65th St., Kansas City, Mo. 64133.*

Lawrence Okrend

Ray Lawler demonstrates spiral cutting. The travel of the slide rest is controlled by the brass gears mounted on the headstock.

Lawrence Okrend

Lawler's new ornamental lathe is larger and more convenient to operate than its 18th- and 19th-century ancestors. An electric motor, rather than foot-powered treadle, drives the headstock as well as the overhead counterweighted pulleys which operate cutting frames mounted on a slide rest on the lathe bed. Brass gears mounted on the headstock (right) drive the work and the slide rest for spiraling. Hundreds of indexing holes in the gears and brass pulleys position work for making a staggering variety of patterns with the machine's cutting frames.

Buy the parts, build the bed

by David Sloan

If you've always wanted an extra-long-bed lathe, or one that knocks down for easy hauling to craft shows, this new lathe, designed and built by Conover Woodcraft Specialties (18125 Madison Rd., Parkman, Ohio 44080) is just the thing. For $895, Conover gives you a cast-iron headstock, tailstock, motor bracket and tool-rest assembly (he sells the parts separately, too) designed to mount on a wooden bed. The bed can be long, short, or any style you like, because you build it yourself.

The headstock can swing 16-in.-dia. stock over the bed—larger if you build a gap bed. There's no outboard spindle, but you can slide the headstock out to the end of the bed for turning tabletops and the like, although you'll need to move the motor mount and rig up an outboard

With Conover's new headstock, tailstock and accessories, you can custom-build your own lathe. Instructions for making the plywood bed shown here are given in the manual.

support for the tool rest. The hefty 1½-in.-dia. spindle is fitted with a 4-step pulley. Mounting an additional 4-step pulley on the motor shaft will give you a range of speeds from 600 RPM to 2300 RPM.

For a few weeks, I tried out a borrowed lathe mounted on the glued-up Baltic-birch plywood bed suggested in the owner's manual. The bed was rigid enough for light work, but needed more weight for roughing-

out bowls. Adding a few hundred pounds of sand would solve that problem fast. The lathe itself is good quality and feels solid. □

David Sloan is an associate editor of Fine Woodworking.

Disc Sander Sculpts Turnings

A way to cut spirals without an ornamental lathe

by William Hunter

I am a woodturner, and turning a bowl allows me to search a piece of wood inside and out for the fullest realization of the wood's potential. Sometimes the turned wood is so inherently beautiful that I cannot improve on it. But sometimes the form and figure warrant enrichment. One of my favorite ways to treat such a turning is to put it in motion, that is, to send the eye along a journey over its surface. I groove the bowl in regular or irregular spirals. Then I mount it on an asymmetric stand, a ribbon of wood sculpted to present the sculpted turning.

My method has evolved from 15 years as a sculptor and briar pipe maker. The effect is reminiscent of those formal patterns produced on a Holtzapffel ornamental lathe. But instead of employing mechanized cutters controlled by pulleys, cogs and ratchets, I sit in front of a stationary disc sander and move the piece freehand over the disc's spinning edge.

The method may seem dangerous. But in the several years I ran a five-man shop, and in the several teaching experiences I've had at the high school level, I've never witnessed a run-in with the disc sander that required more than a band-aid to cover a minor strawberry. This is the result of conscientious attention to safe practices: always wear safety glasses with side screens; work in adequate light; use a stable, comfortable stool; wear a dust mask; maintain a concerted mental attitude. The mechanics of this technique are not inherently dangerous. The edge of the disc is not sharp, and disc speed is relatively slow. If you do accidentally touch the disc, centrifugal force throws your hand free. Because there is no table on my setup, there is no chance of pinch or kickback.

I begin such a turning by selecting a piece of wood that, while beautiful in color, is not exceptionally figured. I bandsaw a circular blank, glue it onto a piece of hardwood of the same diameter as the faceplate, using 5-minute epoxy, and screw the glue block to a faceplate. Then I turn the outside of the form between centers and sand completely, from 80-grit down through 400-grit. I find that simple, closed forms work better than open, flared forms. Spheres are easier than spheroids with flat surfaces. In small work, I don't hollow the bowl until the very end.

To lay out a bowl, I first mark the limits of the spiral: With the lathe turning, I press a pencil to the wood ½ in. from the bottom of the bowl and ½ in. from what will be the

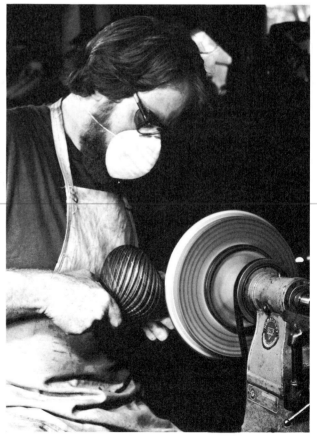

After the outside of a bowl is turned, regular spirals are laid out, above, by pivoting a compass from a block of wood, positioned first on one side, then on the other side of the lathe. A plywood disc mounted outboard indexes the blank. Freehand disc-sculpting, right, requires careful, measured, graceful movements. The sanding disc (which is the same piece of plywood that serves as the indexing wheel for layout) turns only 300 RPM to 500 RPM and is beveled on its back face to yield a definite edge against which the stock is drawn.

Photos: Leroy Radanovich and Bob Barrett

This 8-in. dia. marnut bowl on East Indian rosewood stand looks as if it were made on an ornamental lathe, but the spiral decorations were freehand-carved on the edge of a stationary disc sander.

lip of the bowl. I also make a mark around the bowl's largest diameter. This line will be the point where the spiral changes direction. It is also the circumference around which the spacing of the spirals is marked.

So that the spirals will be spaced evenly, I have mounted on the outboard side of the lathe a 12-in. plywood indexing plate. This plate (marked off in 28, 32, 40 and 48 increments, or however many you want) is a substitute for the lathe's smaller indexing plate. It is screwed to an outboard faceplate, offering a wider choice of indexing patterns and more control over tolerances. A pointer clamped to the lathe stand allows me to hold the bowl in position for each layout line. The spiral offers endless possibilities, but a good place to start is with 12 increments. As many as 24 increments work well on bowls up to 6 in. in diameter. I lay out each spiral with a compass pivoting from a block of wood clamped to the tool rest. Experiment with the compass and various tool-rest positions, looking for a pleasing sweep. Once decided, pencil an arc from the bowl top to the bowl center, crossing through each index mark. Reposition the tool rest on the other side of the lathe to complete the bottom of the arc, from the high point to the foot. Remove the turning, still attached to its faceplate, and examine the scribed lines to make sure that the layout is both accurate and aesthetically pleasing.

Now I move to the disc sander. This is the same plywood disc I have mounted outboard for an indexing plate: I cement 24-grit aluminum oxide (cloth-backed, resin bond) to the outside face and run the lathe at 300 RPM to 500 RPM. The slow speed affords better control for initial cutting, and the large diameter keeps the disc operating cool and also pre-

vents the paper from excessive loading. The edge of the disc is beveled at 30° toward its back side, so that there is a definite edge for cutting precise V-grooves. I cut with the outermost ¼ in. (or less) of the wheel, arcing the stock down along the edge, rather than pushing it straight in. I aim my cuts between the lines, trying to leave the pencil lines intact as reference until I approach finish-sanding. Disc-sculpting requires careful, measured, graceful movements, so it is important that you are seated comfortably, that your posture is relaxed and that your workspace is well lighted. Grip and wrist motion must be consistent so that all passes are equal. Therefore, you must maintain total concentration, without interruptions.

The first cut is very shallow and defines the basic form of the groove. Go once around the whole bowl, cutting about ⅟₁₆ in. deep in each groove. The second pass cuts deeper and wider into the established groove. You are now committed. Sometimes it takes only two passes to cut the desired arcs, sometimes as many as five. In this phase it is essential that each cut be equal and in sequence—never backtrack. Irregularities are better worked out with finer grits. It is also important to keep clear of the top and bottom guidelines; taper out the grooves later, with a finer-grit disc.

In the next phase I use an 8-in. Power Pad (available through Power Pad Mfg., 1223 W. 256th St., Harbor City, Calif. 90710) to refine form and to remove scratches. This is an industrial-quality foam disc that's flexible enough to sand contours easily. It's available in soft, medium and hard consistencies; I use mostly soft and medium. I cut my own sanding discs for the Power Pad from aluminum oxide and silicon carbide paper. It's less expensive than using pre-cut discs, but,

After the grooves are cut on the plywood sanding disc, Hunter uses a foam-backed disc to refine the shapes.

more important, you can control the amount of overhang. I use somewhere between ¹⁄₃₂-in. and ¼-in. overhang, depending on whether I'm going for a hard line or a soft, rolled effect. Usually, ⅛ in. is preferable. Also, after I cut an 8-in. disc out of 8½-in. by 11-in. paper, I am left with enough scraps to use for lathe sanding and drum sanders. I recycle discs worn at the perimeter by cutting them down for 5-in. Power Pads and orbital sander discs.

I sand each groove in sequence, going two or three times around the bowl with the Power Pad in each grit. I begin with 80-grit aluminum oxide paper, then repeat the process with 150-grit aluminum oxide, 220-grit aluminum oxide and 400-grit silicon carbide. Then I move to the Sand-O-Flex flap sander (which can also be run on the lathe), using a combination of 240-grit and 320-grit, ⅛-in. shred, for removal of sharp edges and concave finish work. Final-sanding is done on the Power Pad, with 400-grit and 600-grit, then I hand-sand. The piece is now ready for buffing.

The buffing process I use was originally designed for briar smoking pipes and works well on closed-grain hardwoods. The beauty of it is that, unlike metal buffing compounds, it

does not clog the pores of the wood and it tones but does not discolor hardwoods. It is quick, and it burnishes the wood, adds luster and depth, and produces a hard, gem-like finish.

I use buffing wheels, compounds and waxes available from Pimo Pipe Supplies, Box 59211, Chicago, Ill. 60659. The wheels, designed for pipemakers, have a beveled edge that allows more detail in buffing. I generally use a 1-in. wide beveled buffing wheel, 9 in. in diameter. Wider wheels work best on broad surfaces because they provide a consistent polish with less danger of removing soft areas in the wood's surface. All of these wheels are designed to run at 1725 RPM, either with a ½-HP motor or on the lathe. The compounds are colored waxes—green, red and white—impregnated with abrasive grits equal to 700-, 800- and 900-grit. I use four wheels. The first is a firm sewn muslin, which I use with green compound. The second is a softer sewn flannel, used with red compound. The third, a soft unsewn flannel, is used with white compound. The fourth, a very soft flannel, is for the hard carnauba wax. It is important not to overload the wheels with abrasives.

If all has gone well, you now have a spiraled bowl, the exterior of which is complete. Time now to return to the lathe to hollow the bowl. I prefer a closed form for my spiral-grooved turnings because it allows me greater surface area to explore sculptural techniques.

I find it helpful to begin with a ¾-in. drill bit in the tailstock, to clear the center and define the bottom of the piece. I hollow-turn with a combination of handmade chisels, using a spear point for clearing waste and a roundnose for finishing. (Hollow turning with bent tools is especially interesting with crotches, butts and burls.) After I'm satisfied with wall thickness, usually ⅛ in. to ¼ in., and the last chisel cut is smooth, I cut the bowl from the faceplate, beginning with a parting tool and finishing with a backsaw. I finish the bottom on the disc and belt sanders.

Freehand disc-sculpting is workmanship of risk. It takes hundreds of passes with the disc's edge before you capture the spiral and you hold the finished form in your hands. Then you feel its weight for the first time, to know the thickness of its walls, and the piece comes to life. □

Freehand disc-sanding also lends itself to less regular, asymmetric decoration, as in this 6-in. dia. Indian rosewood bowl.

Bill Hunter is a professional turner in El Portal, Calif.

An answer to breathing dust

Turning tropical woods, fossilized walrus tusks, soapstone and amber was a health hazard in my shop. Solving the problem has been quite a challenge.

First I set up an exhaust system built out of parts from an old line-finisher (a shoe repair bar). These machines are outdated in the shoe industry and can be picked up relatively cheap: $100 to $200 (1983 prices). They have a great 6-in. exhaust system built in. I cannibalized the one from our machine, and hooked it up to a 1½-HP motor and 6-in. stovepipe. This handled most of the dust from my lathe, but some left the force field, especially during power-sanding. So I experimented with a box, as shown in the drawing, that totally enclosed the headstock, the tool rest and the piece, yet still allowed work on the piece. For most turning, the box, in conjunction with the line-shaft exhaust system, worked. There are some drawbacks, however. You need several sizes for different scale work, power-sanding is possible only awkwardly through the top, vision is limited, and the setup slows you down. Also, for turning soapstone (with its high asbestos content) and fossilized walrus tusk (which I'm highly allergic to), I needed more protection—I could still see small amounts of dust escaping. The lathe box is close to what I need, and I regard it as a must, so I'm still trying to improve it.

Meanwhile, I sought advice through the occupational safety program at San Francisco General Hospital. For only $15, a team of experts, both medical and industrial, spent an evening discussing my problem with me. Two weeks later I received a package of safety information, including specs on the 3M Airhat (available from Direct Safety, Box 8018, Phoenix, Ariz. 85040).

To be absolutely assured with this system, you have to get a licensed industrial safety engineer to come and test the particulate content of your shop. The cost of such a test was almost the cost of the $400 Airhat, so I took the chance, figuring that if I had no allergic reaction when working walrus ivory, I would be adequately protected against other substances as well.

The Airhat includes a protective Lexan face shield, a beard collar, an air hose, and a battery and filter pump you wear on your belt. In conjunction with my lathe box and exhaust system it works great. I had *no* allergic reaction to walrus tusk at all. I have found the system as comfortable as a face shield, and I prefer it to a dual-filter respirator and

goggles. The helmet has several adjustments for proper fit. The battery pack and pump are light and behind you, out of the way. The hum of the pump isn't a problem; after a couple of minutes it seems to go away. I also wear a lab coat now, so *all* dust is left in the shop.

In my opinion, here are the positive aspects of the Airhat:
—It provides total face protection, even if you wear a beard, and partial head protection from "fly-off."
—There's no facial pressure or sweat as with a respirator-and-goggle combination; it's actually cool and pleasantly breezy inside.
—I've had no fogging problem.
—It provides dust protection in shop areas that don't have exhaust.
—Talking is easier than in a dust mask.
—It doesn't interfere with large ear protectors or eyeglasses.
—It's been easy to maintain and clean.
—You feel secure and healthy inside it.

Dust-free and breezy inside his 3M Airhat, Hunter turns a bowl in the dust-collection box drawn below.

Working materials like the ivory of this 4½-in. dia. bowl requires special attention to dust collection.

Here are the negative aspects:
—It costs $400.
—Its batteries need to be charged for 12 to 16 hours after every 8 hours of operation. You'll damage them if you "top off" the charge frequently. An extra battery can be ordered, but this still requires orderly attention.
—It takes longer to put on and take off than other respirators, and it's tough to train yourself to use it *all the time.*
—You sound weird on the phone.
—Shop partners have a tough time taking you seriously.

I highly recommend the Airhat in conjunction with some form of shop exhaust system. I've had no experience in a totally dust-filled room using only an Airhat. —*W.H.*

Lathe box for dust collection

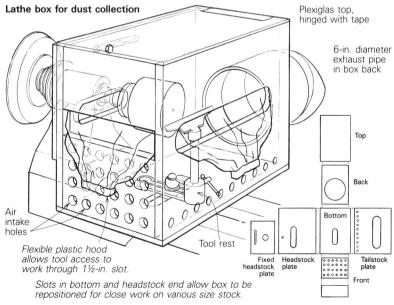

Plexiglas top, hinged with tape

6-in. diameter exhaust pipe in box back

Top

Back

Bottom

Front

Fixed headstock plate

Headstock plate

Tailstock plate

Tool rest

Air intake holes

Flexible plastic hood allows tool access to work through 1½-in. slot.

Slots in bottom and headstock end allow box to be repositioned for close work on various size stock.

Drawing: Lee Hov

Twist Turning
Traditional method combines lathe and carving

by Eric Schramm

Spiral or twist turning was introduced in Europe during the 16th century and was used widely for chair and table legs in 17th-century England. Today, the technique finds uses in antique reproduction and repair and for the Mediterranean-style furniture popular in the Southwest and West.

Spirals, solid and hollow, are not turnings in the true sense of the word because most of the work is really carving. A spiral resembles a screw thread; it has pitch and lead. Pitch is the distance from center to center of consecutive ridges or bines. Lead is the distance the spiral advances along the cylinder in each revolution. In a single-twist spiral, pitch and lead are the same. A spiral with a short pitch and great depth will be weak because much of the long-grain wood has been removed. A longer pitch will be stronger but less pleasing to the eye. I find that a pitch about equal to or slightly less than the cylinder's diameter produces the nicest effect. The precise pitch, however, is governed by cylinder length, if the spiral bines are to be spaced equally and are to start and finish their lead symmetrically.

To lay out a single spiral, you must divide the cylinder's circumference into four equal parts. A quick method is to wrap a strip of paper around the circumference and trim it so the ends just meet. Remove the paper and fold it in half once, and then in half again. The fold marks, which will quarter the cylinder, can be transferred directly to the workpiece with a pencil. With the cylinder on the lathe and the tool rest acting as a straightedge, draw four lines along the length of the workpiece passing through these marks (figure 1a).

Next divide the cylinder's length into spaces that are equal to or slightly less than the cylinder diameter (figure 1b). These marks are the pitch lines and represent the distance between the spiral's ridges. Pitch lines drawn, divide the space between them into four equal spaces. You can now sketch the spiral ridge by drawing a continuous line diagonally through one after another of the quarter spaces between the pitch lines. A scrap of sandpaper makes a good straightedge (figure 1c) for drawing the diagonal lines. If you've done things properly, the ridge line will cross a pitch line with each revolution. With the ridge line completed, draw in another line parallel to it to roughly locate the spiral's groove. The ridge line will remain intact through the carving process.

A double spiral, the most popular form, is layed out similarly. The pitch remains the same, but the lead doubles. So this time, divide the space between pitch lines into two instead of four sections. Draw one ridge line as before, passing diagonally through the squares. In the length of one diameter, this ridge line will traverse 180°. Start a second ridge line 180° from the first, and draw the diagonals so the line remains 180° from the first throughout the length of the cylinder. Triple spirals can be plotted by dividing the circumference into six parts and starting the ridge lines at 120° intervals.

Ridge lines can be drawn also by wrapping a strip of paper around the turning, leaving a slight space between turns. A pencil line is then traced through the spiral space.

Actual cutting of the spiral is tedious but not difficult. First make a saw cut on the line that represents the bottom of the groove. Start with a saw with a strip of wood clamped to it or some masking tape to indicate the depth of cut, which should be about a quarter of the workpiece diameter (photo A). Rotate the work slowly while cutting so the kerf will follow the line. After sawing, the space between the bines is shaped by making broad V-cuts with a sharp chisel or No. 2 carver's gouge (photo B). Use a round file to clean up these spaces (photo C), then dress up the rounds with a flat cabinet file. The spiral can be rotated in the lathe by hand to permit longer file strokes and smoother results. Preserve the ridge line throughout. Finish with sandpaper, or use a shop-made pinwheel sander (make 8-vaned pinwheels, like the child's toy, from sandpaper; secure on arbor and chuck in lathe or drill).

Another variation of the double or triple spiral is the hollow spiral where the bines of the spiral are separated by an opening. Hollow or open spirals generally lack sufficient strength for furniture legs, but are quite effective as candlesticks or lamp bases. The work is layed out as for the double or triple spiral, with the cutting line that represents the bottom of the groove used as a drilling line. A V-block is used when drilling to assure accuracy (photo D). The holes go through the turning and are best drilled half way through from each side to avoid splintering. Finish the shape with chisels, files and sandpaper (photo E). One of the best tools for cleaning out the inside is an ordinary sharp carving knife. Irregularities and tool marks can be removed with strips of sanding belt, pulled back and forth around the bines (photo F). Make the final strokes in the direction of the grain. A great deal of patience and skill is required for neat work. The wood used should be tough, hard, and free from defects.

Tapered spirals for flame finials are also possible. To lay out a taper, you must make the pitch vary so that it equals the diminishing diameter of the workpiece. Begin as above by striking four lines along the length of the taper. Then measure the diameter of the taper's large end and mark this distance on one of the four longitudinal lines. At this mark, measure the diameter again and mark this length along the taper. Repeat this process until you reach the end of the cylinder. Adjust the various pitch lines you have drawn so that they diminish proportionally. Draw in the ridge line and proceed with the cuts as in straight work. To make a flame finial, draw four ridge lines starting at 90° intervals from the large end of the taper. Use double ridge lines about ⅛ in. apart, and use gouges and files to remove the waste. I find a Moto Tool with a round burr a good tool for forming the flame. □

Eric Schramm designs and builds custom furniture in Los Gatos, Calif. Photos by Robert Schramm.

From *Fine Woodworking* magazine (March 1982) 33:92-93

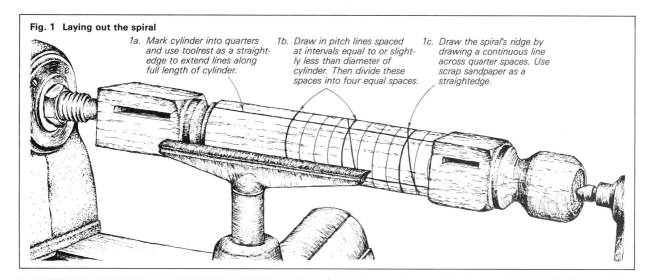

Fig. 1 Laying out the spiral

1a. Mark cylinder into quarters and use toolrest as a straight-edge to extend lines along full length of cylinder.

1b. Draw in pitch lines spaced at intervals equal to or slightly less than diameter of cylinder. Then divide these spaces into four equal spaces.

1c. Draw the spiral's ridge by drawing a continuous line across quarter spaces. Use scrap sandpaper as a straightedge.

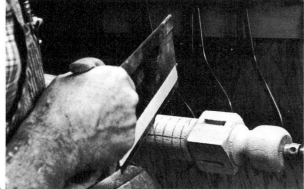

A

With the layout complete, use a backsaw to cut the initial kerf which will serve as a guide for carving the spiral's grooves.

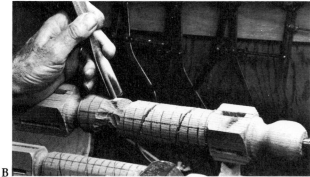

B

Shaping the spiral is hard work. Start with a chisel or No. 2 carver's gouge. You can control the shape of the grooves and ridges by varying the angle of your chisel cuts.

C

After carving, use rasps and sandpaper to form the spiral in the shape you want. Here, sandpaper is wrapped around a rasp that acts as a sanding block to maintain the radius.

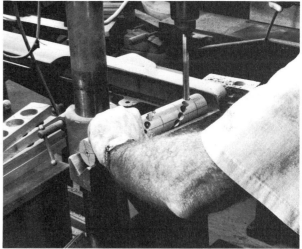

D

The hollow spiral layout is identical to that of the solid spiral. To waste the center of a hollow spiral, Schramm uses a drill press with the stock anchored against turning and slipping by a V-block.

E

After the drill press, it's back to carving by hand. The final shape of the hollow spiral is done with chisels, knives, rasps and sandpaper. Lathe-mounting allows the work to be positioned while carving.

F

Cloth-backed sanding paper holds up well for sanding the bines of a hollow spiral. Old sanding belts can be cut into strips for this job. Use progressively finer grits to get a good finish.

A Mechanical Twist

The tablesaw can be used to lay out a helix and to cut its initial kerf at the same time. Then with a molding head on the saw and a guide pin running in that kerf, the bulk of the waste can be machined away. The basic method is to clamp an angled fence across the saw table just ahead of the sawblade, which is raised only ¼ in. above the table surface. A blank cylinder, lodged against the table and the fence and rotated over the blade, will feed itself along the fence regularly and automatically. The result is a helical kerf whose pitch is governed by the angle of the fence. A cylinder turned between square pommels, what you'd want for chair or table legs, can also be tablesawn in this way by screwing free-spinning end-blocks onto the stock, as shown at right. The end-blocks raise the stock off the table and away from the fence so its square sections don't interfere with its rotation.

As in all twist turning, the first step is to turn the blank cylinder, straight or between square pommels, depending on the application. There's uncertainty in these procedures so make five blanks if you need four legs. Then choose the pitch angle (α), which determines how quickly the helix rises—that is, its pitch, or lead, how far apart its ridges are. A pitch angle around 18° saws a helix whose lead (L) about equals its diameter (D). This pitch angle is set by locking the miter gauge at 72° (that is, 90° minus 18°), and using the gauge to locate the fence on the saw table. Whatever the angle, the fence should be located so that the center of the blank cylinder is directly above the center of the sawblade. Moving the fence forward or backward has the same effect as changing its angle. To saw a double helix whose ridges are still one diameter apart, use a pitch angle around 32°, which means set the miter gauge at 58°. Pitch angle (α), diameter (D) and lead (L) can be figured with the following formula:

$$\tan \alpha = \frac{L}{\pi D}$$

Always use a sturdy fence that's more than twice as long as the stock—a length of 2x4 is good. When the fence slopes away from the operator from right to left, the resulting helix will be like a left-handed thread. When the fence slopes away from left to right, the helix will be right-handed. Always feed the stock from the near side of the sawblade (the downhill side), always rotate it against the sawblade's rotation (so the blade doesn't self-feed), and always keep your hands well clear of the blade's path. For a double spiral, start the second kerf at a point 180° opposite the first.

After the helical kerf is cut, you can remount the stock on the lathe for carving, or you can further shape it with the molding head. Use coving knives in the head, and make a snugly fitting wooden insert for the tablesaw throat. Set a small dowel in the face of the fence (photo), just long enough to catch in the kerf. Fit this fence pin into the kerf and use the miter gauge (set as before) to locate the stock in relation to a molding knife. Clamp the fence to the saw table and rotate the stock into the molding head, slowly and carefully. The pin will automatically feed the stock. Shaping with the molding head has to be done in one pass because the cut removes the guide kerf. After the molding knives have done what they can, the helix can be cleaned up with carving tools, rasps and sandpaper. A strip of cloth-backed sandpaper in a bowsaw frame will speed the chore.   —*Larry Green*

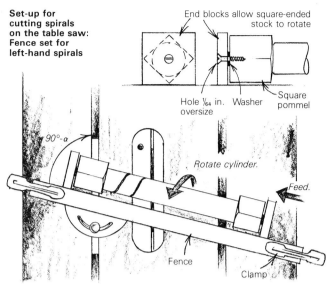

Set-up for cutting spirals on the table saw: Fence set for left-hand spirals

End blocks allow square-ended stock to rotate

Hole ¹⁄₆₄ in. oversize · Washer · Square pommel

90°-α · Rotate cylinder. · Feed. · Fence · Clamp

Position fence so stock center and saw arbor are vertically in line. Use miter gauge to set fence angle. Raise sawblade to cut ¼ in. into cylinder. Free-spinning endblocks provide clearance for square pommels, as shown in the detail at top.

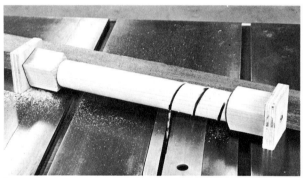

Rotate cylinder into the sawblade to cut helical kerf, above. It will feed itself along the angled fence.

Dowel pin set in fence will guide kerfed cylinder past molding head (right). Cut must be deep because a second cut is not possible (below). Go slowly to minimize tear-out.

From *Fine Woodworking* magazine (March 1982) 33:94

A Portfolio of Spirals

When he was in elementary school, Mark Phenicie saw a vine-festooned tree with a naturally spiraled trunk that inspired him to try making a spiral himself. Phenicie, of Berwyn, Pa., has been at it ever since. He carves hollow spirals with as many as six separate bines winding about the cylinder, and he sometimes adds V-grooves to the face of the bines for further embellishment. Phenicie's spirals go into making decorative accessories such as the pedestal plant stand in the photo at left and furniture components like the coffee table legs and stretcher pictured above. Instead of drawing the spiral's ridge line directly on the stock, Phenicie covers the cylinder in masking tape first. He then cuts away the masking tape where the spiral's groove will be and he uses the remaining tape as a guideline when cutting out the center of the spiral. Instead of drilling out the waste, Phenicie uses a router. He leaves the work in his lathe and routs out the grooves with a series of shallow cuts, turning the work by hand to better position the router. Since the router usually lacks sufficient depth to completely hollow the spiral, Phenicie uses a Surform tool to finish the hollowing and to rough out the bines. He uses cloth-backed sandpaper to smooth the spiral's final shape. Photos: Mark Phenicie.

Fred Johnson of Andover, Mass., used the drill-press method to hollow the spiral for this pedestal table. He used a keyhole saw, rasps, rifflers and 'sheet upon sheet' of sandpaper to finish the piece. Photo: Fred Johnson.

J.R. Thomas of Cerrillos, N.M. designs spirals into his Spanish-influence furniture. But he doesn't use fancy formulas or complicated layouts to make them. "I just screw around with a bevel gauge until I get something that pleases my eye," Thomas says. The pieces shown here were done for a Santa Fe builder. Thomas carves his spirals entirely with V-gouges and in-cannels. He puts all the legs for a piece in his vise, carves them at once on the square stock, and finishes each individually with rasps and sandpaper. Photo: J.R. Thomas.

WOODTURNING ON A METAL LATHE

Is there something different about Michelle Holzapfel's turned work? One turner, after learning how a piece was made, thought it appeared mechanical. She agrees: "My work has changed since I picked up this method. It has a removed quality which I like."

When Holzapfel first encountered the lathe, she knew she had found her craft. She began developing skills with the woodturner's usual selection of tools—keep the bevel rubbing, lift the handle, roll the tool, swing the handle. It's frustrating learning a delicate craft from books. "I can remember a few times having the feeling of being in control," she said, "but the effort to cut correctly diverted my energy from making the shape I wanted."

Holzapfel's lathe was assembled by her machinist father from odd parts, and it includes the cross slide and compound that metal-lathe operators use

for precision work. When she tried these controls for shaping wood, she put her hand tools away forever.

Remember the drawing toy you had as a kid, with a screen and two little knobs? One knob made the stylus move up or down, the other moved it right or left, and you wound up with a sketch that looked like an etching. Remember the frustration in trying to draw a curved line? It took heroic concentration yet everything still came out with jagged corners. Controls on a machinist's lathe work the same way. The cutting tool is mounted rigidly in the mechanism and moved at right angles to the lathe bed by the cross-slide crank. The compound crank controls longitudinal movements. Holzapfel moves the controls simultaneously and independently to develop the graceful curves usually associated with freehand turning.

Many of us who turn wood are in love

with the dance, those odd contortions we perform that echo the evolving shape on the lathe. Holzapfel's turning is more cerebral. She stands quietly in deep concentration, twirling a couple of cranks. Her control is as sure as any hand-turner's and her work is as fine. But she is free of worry about the tool digging in or catching in a crevice. "At first I missed the flexibility of using hand tools," she said, "but within a matter of days the machinery just fell away. I have no thought of bevels rubbing or anything but where the edge is and where I want it to be. I'm really free to concentrate on the shape.

"Because I don't have to hold the tool, I don't get tired. If I alternate sitting and standing, I can work eight, nine, ten hours a day."

Instead of the risk of working freehand, Holzapfel savors the adventure of working burls, crotches and spalted wood. Though her pieces are elegantly formed and superbly polished (two rubbed coats of tung oil and a third left to set on the surface), a bowl's contour may be interrupted by included bark, or the eye may be distracted from the delicate shape of a plate by a random spalt pattern. It is a harmonious discord that gives Holzapfel's work its vitality. "If a piece of wood is flawless," she said, "I don't know what to do with it. Working perfect wood bores me to tears."

With her husband, David, Holzapfel shares a shop, two children and a basic approach to wood. He makes tables of wildly shaped slabs in what he calls an "aformal" style. Their showroom in Marlboro, Vt., is called "Applewood," the translation of their German name.

"We have a common philosophy taking off in two completely different directions," said Michelle. "David believes in real randomness while I want to formalize things. But we both try to let the wood talk to us."

Reflecting on her technique, Holzapfel believes that handicapped persons could use it to gain access to turning. "A handicap is just a limitation. In a way, I consider myself handicapped. I can't build enough muscle to turn with hand tools for hours. I would have given up turning long ago, but through sheer luck I came upon a way." □

The drive system of Holzapfel's lathe, above, harks back to the days of steam and lineshafts. The motor is mounted below the headstock and drives a jack shaft by means of a belt. The jackshaft drives a second shaft above it, and pulleys on the two give twin speed ranges. The upper shaft has a four-step pulley that mates with a counterpart on the headstock shaft giving a total of eight speeds. An idler on the belt works through a ratcheted lever to engage and disengage the lathe from the motor. The idler will also work as a slip-clutch, allowing very low speeds when revving up heavy, eccentric chunks. Instead of hand-held gouges and skews, Holzapfel grinds her own tools from tool-steel blanks. Pictured at right are a parting tool, a left-hand cutter and a right-hand cutter. Each tool has its own holder. The tools, say Holzapfel, stay sharper longer than hand tools and require only a touch-up on the grinder once a week.

Richard Starr is author of Woodworking with Kids *(The Taunton Press).*

Chucking up odd-shaped pieces, Holzapfel rounds them off as quickly as most turners would with hand tools. Standing to the side, above, keeps her out of the path of flying chips. Rounding off at low speeds, she runs the lathe slowly and since it's bolted to the floor, vibration is minimal.

Holzapfel uses a diamond-point tool, top, to shape a cherry vase. Having become accustomed to the machinist's lathe, she finds it easy to trace a contour while reducing its diameter, a feat of considerable coordination with a compound tool rest. Above, she uses a left-hand cutter to shape a vase's flaring top. Cross slides and compounds are available for many woodturning lathes and old metal lathes of all sizes can be adapted for woodturning.

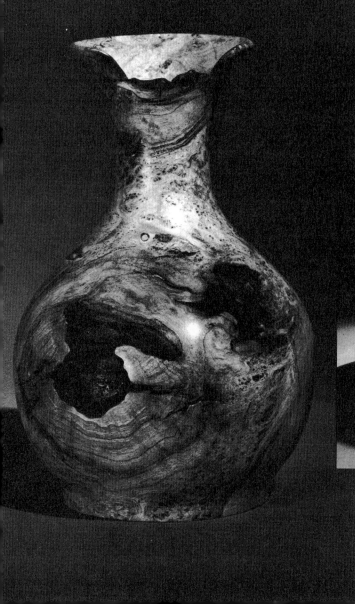

The finest wooden turnings are possible on the metal lathe. At left, the vase's flare was intentionally interrupted by included defects, as was the thin-walled bowl, above. Metal-working tools leave fine ridges which can be removed quickly by 60-grit sandpaper. Holzapfel sands down to 600 grit before applying a tung-oil finish.

Robert Yorgey's Hand-Carved Turnings
Making do with what you have

by Richard Starr

When Robert Yorgey shows his drop-leaf tables at a craft fair, people stop to admire the neatly turned legs and stretchers. But Yorgey didn't use a lathe to form the pretty vase and ring shapes; he carved them by hand. At 85, he's been at it for thirteen years.

"My granddad was a woodworker," says Yorgey. "Maybe I inherited something from him. He used to make the wooden screws and gears for the old forges, the old steel-rolling mills. That was back in the 1850s and 60s. He died around 1906—I was about 10 years old.

"My first encounter with woodworking was when I was 12 or 13. I attempted to make a boomerang, having read about them in some book. It was supposed to return to the thrower. Result was, when I threw it, it kept going. If I were superstitious, I'd believe it was coming back in my carvings now."

Yorgey lives near Reading, Pa., on the farm he has worked for most of his life. "When I sold the farm to my son in 1968, I called it 'I retired,' but I really didn't. I kept on working. I don't believe in that retirement business." Though still busy, he found time to take up woodworking.

One of his early projects was a magazine rack illustrated in William Klenke's book, *Things to Make and How to Make Them*. The rack had four short, delicately turned legs. "I had Klenke's book, but the only hitch was, I didn't have a lathe. Klenke didn't tell me one thing: how to do it with hand tools." Yorgey describes himself as being of "tough Pennsylvania Dutch stock." True to this, he carved the turned shapes with a chisel, a gouge, a coping saw, a Surform and a good deal of careful measurement. The results were convincing and pleasing. He was encouraged to try a more complex piece from Klenke's book: a gate-leg table.

"Listen, my first table I made all by hand. There was a walnut log up in the woods, 7 ft. long by 7 in. It was lying over and was pretty dry and I got it in the old summer kitchen, and I sawed it with a handsaw. Full length. It took me about two days to saw one trip through. I sawed it out in about 2-in. planks." He ripped the planks into 2x2s for the eight legs and six stretchers. Each piece was "turned" by hand using carving tools, with the work held in a vise.

Yorgey has made 22 gate-leg and trestle-style drop-leaf tables in a variety of local woods—cherry, walnut, butternut and dogwood—all with hand-turned parts. Each tabletop has its own corner shape. "I try to put different corners and colors in each table so I can say it's pretty near one of a kind." He

Graceful symmetry of Yorgey's table legs in dogwood belies its lathe-less origins.

carves the rule joint between the main top and the drop-leaf by hand and judges the quality of the table partly by how well this joint fits. "See, this one I didn't get quite as good as those; I don't get them all perfect. These latest ones I got pretty good because I had a little more experience."

With experience came the need to diversify. "I don't know what branched me off to the vises. I guess I wanted a challenge. The gate-leg tables weren't enough of a challenge for me." Yorgey cuts the wooden screws and nuts for his vises by hand. He uses a short piece of metal tape-measure as a flexible layout ruler, and carves the threads with a V-gouge. To make the nuts, he drills a hole in a block of wood, then saws the block in half through the hole. After gouging out the threads, he glues the block back together. Though Yorgey developed his own threading technique, it closely resembles the procedure described by Hero of Alexandria almost two thousand years ago. When simple vises were no longer challenging enough, Yorgey designed and built a vise whose moving jaw floats on a pair of opposite-threaded screws that are coupled together by wooden gears. Improved variations are now in the works.

Yorgey was invited to demonstrate his unique style of non-lathe turning at two symposia held in Newtown, Pa., in 1979 (see p. 83 for more on the June session). Surrounded by 20 growling lathes, he quietly chipped out screws and table parts, attracting a good deal of amused, though respectful, attention. "They were ribbing me about taking too much time and patience doing this. So I had to get back at them. I told them, 'I'm the original. You fellows are all copiers!'" Yorgey's message has a certain authenticity to it: perhaps the lathe was originally developed to mimic hand-carved objects. When he was reminded that the lathe is a very ancient tool, Yorgey replied, "Before the lathe were my tools."

Robert Yorgey came to his craft late in life; perhaps that explains the joy with which he works. But why the unusual methods? "You just want to try to see what you can do with what you have," he says. "Here's another reason; maybe you'll agree with me and maybe you won't. I went through the Depression and I guess that knocked a little patience in me, and a little endurance too." ☐

Richard Starr, of Thetford Center, Vt., is author of Woodworking with Kids, *available from The Taunton Press.*

From *Fine Woodworking* magazine (May 1981) 28:84-85

With the work held in twin-screw vise, Yorgey shapes a leg with a Surform.

Yorgey at home with four of his gate-leg tables.

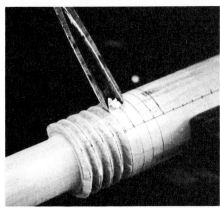

Yorgey lays out his screw threads with a flexible ruler and carves them with a V-gouge (above, left). The result is a spiral with a pitch of four to the inch. Nuts are similarly roughed out with gouge and mallet, left, but the stock must be drilled and halved first and the threads must meet when the halves are re-assembled. The finished twin-screw vise, above, is a monument to skill, patience and leisure time. Crank mounted on top screw is geared to opposite-threaded lower screw. Rear jaw has two threaded holes and moves on the screws as the crank is turned. Because simple wooden gears would be too coarse to work smoothly and finer gears would be too fragile, Yorgey mounted two gears on each screw, one-half tooth out of phase. The effect is as smooth as single gears with twice as many teeth, but is far stronger.

Photos: Richard Starr

Turning Without a Lathe

Working in the round with handtools

by Aldren A. Watson and Theodora A. Poulos

Making turned legs without a lathe isn't complex and you can obtain good results with ordinary handtools. Because these tools require considerable force and both hands are needed to control them effectively, you must hold the work securely and safe from damage while you're shaping it. The lathebox, shown in figure 1, is the most practical answer.

The lathebox can be built from inexpensive lumber, and it will support turning stock up to 3-in. square and 34½-in. long. You can leave the stock free to rotate or lock it in place with wedges and square blocks or V-shaped blocks. The blocks shown in this box fit the 1⅛-in. squares used to make legs for a pine dressing table (see sidebar, p. 79). For long pieces, like canopy bedposts, you can attach separate head and tail blocks to your bench and add free-standing square or V-blocks, as shown in figure 1. The lathebox is handier for smaller pieces because you can move it without disturbing the work when you need the bench for another job.

To make the dressing table legs, or any similar furniture parts, first trace the pattern (see figure 2, p. 77) on all four faces of the stock, then drive a nail into each end of the piece to serve as mounting spindles in the lathebox. Next, with a chisel shape the stock square in section to the outlines of the traced pattern. Then with chisel, drawknife, spokeshave and file, make the square forms octagonal and, finally, round. The key to success is to do one section of the turning at a time. Take light cuts and carefully follow your layout lines.

Begin by cutting the legs, adding 2 in. to the length for waste. The waste sections protect the finished ends, and serve as reference points for checking your work. Before you begin the actual shaping, drill the holes for the drawbore pins (wooden pegs that will hold the joints together)

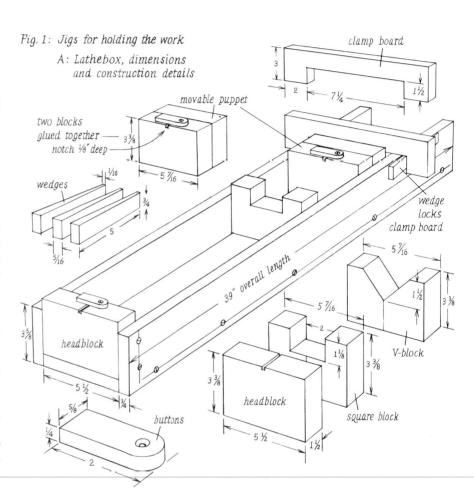

Fig. 1: Jigs for holding the work

A: Lathebox, dimensions and construction details

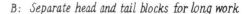

B: Separate head and tail blocks for long work

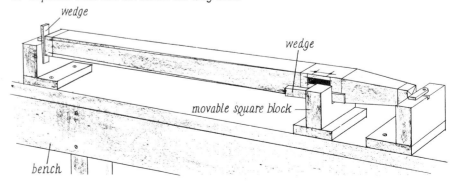

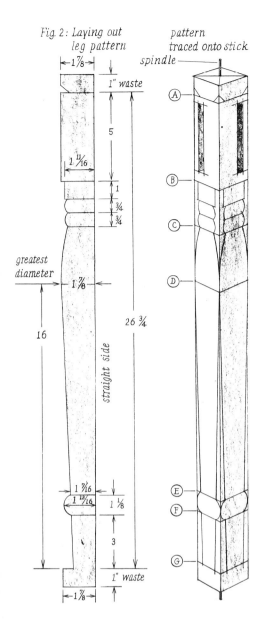

Fig. 2: Laying out leg pattern

pattern traced onto stick

spindle

1 7/8

1" waste

5

1 11/16

1

3/4

3/4

greatest diameter

1 7/8

26 3/4

16

straight side

1 7/16

1 13/16

1 1/8

3

1" waste

1 7/8

Ⓐ

Ⓑ

Ⓒ

Ⓓ

Ⓔ

Ⓕ

Ⓖ

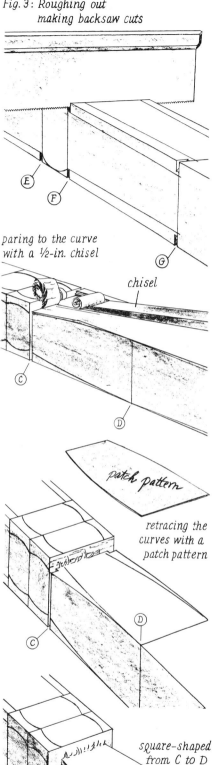

Fig. 3: Roughing out making backsaw cuts

Ⓔ

Ⓕ

Ⓖ

paring to the curve with a 1/2-in. chisel

chisel

Ⓒ

Ⓓ

patch pattern

retracing the curves with a patch pattern

Ⓒ

Ⓓ

square-shaped from C to D

Ⓒ

Ⓓ

and chop the mortises shown in the plan. This is more easily done while the work is flat and square, and it avoids damaging the finished turning.

After cutting the mortises, draw diagonal lines on both ends of each leg to locate the centers, then drive an 8d finish nail about ¾ in. into each center. Cut off the heads with heavy wirecutters or a hacksaw to form ¾-in. spindles. Now mark off the 1-in. waste sections and tape the leg pattern to the work, aligning the straight side of the pattern with one edge of the stock. Use a sharp, soft pencil to trace the pattern from top to bottom. Remove the pattern, flop it over, and tape it down aligned with the other edge of same face. Trace the pattern onto all four sides, then use a try square to draw the reference lines A, B, C, D, E, F, and G, again on all four sides.

Put the work in the lathebox, twist the

buttons over the spindles and drive wedges into the clampboard to secure the movable puppet or tailstock. After securing the box in your vise, outline the leg sections by making light backsaw cuts 1/16-in. deep on all four sides at B, C, E, F and G. To prevent tearout, saw across the corners first, then level the saw to complete the cuts (figure 3). While sawing, secure the leg with blocks and a wedge between the stock and the headblock.

Begin the actual shaping between C and D. With a ½-in. chisel held bevel-up, pare off wood following the curved lines, using hand pressure alone (no mallet). Take thin, narrow slices, which are easier to control than great wide cuts. Pare close to the lines, but leave them showing. It is especially important not to lose the reference lines at D, which mark the greatest diameter of the leg.

After shaping the first side, make a small patch pattern as shown, and retrace the pencil lines you removed with the wood, so that you can shape the second side. The small patch pattern is easier to align than the whole pattern. Rotate the work in the lathebox and shape the opposing side in the same way. Repeat for the remaining two sides.

Next, deepen the saw cuts on all four sides at E and F (both sides of the bulb). Then use a ½-in. chisel to cut pockets on all four sides of the leg above E, below F, and at G. These pockets establish square sections that serve as reference points as you continue shaping the leg.

A drawknife efficiently roughs out the long taper between D and E. For best control, hold the knife bevel-down and slice at an angle to the length of the leg. Shave thin slices rather than heavy splinters and frequently check the layout lines. As the work progresses, snug up wedges securing the square block and V-block as needed. You can smooth the surfaces with a spokeshave. A small bull-nose plane will get into the tight spots just above E, or you can pare carefully with a 1-in. chisel held bevel-up. Try to keep the sides of the taper as nearly square as possible, or it will be difficult to make the leg octagonal in the next step. Check for squareness by measuring in from the untouched faces at E and by sliding a try square along each of the four sides. Also, set a straightedge along the length of each side to check for humps or hollows. Pencil-mark any high spots, then shave off the marks with a spoke-shave or block plane.

Next, rough-shape the bulb. Lay out

Fig. 4: Shaping the bulb, octagon dimension for bulb

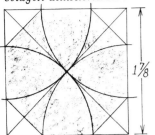

$1\frac{7}{8}$

To layout an octagon, first draw a square. Set a compass to the distance from one corner of the square to the center. Draw arcs from each corner. Their intersections with the sides of the square mark the eight angles of an octagon.

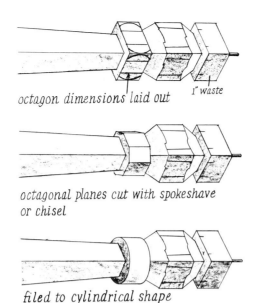

octagon dimensions laid out

1" waste

octagonal planes cut with spokeshave or chisel

filed to cylindrical shape

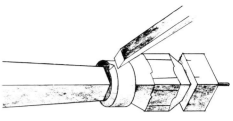

beveling with $\frac{3}{8}$" chisel and light mallet

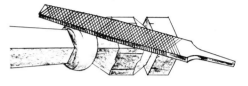

rounding with double cut file

---

lines on all four sides $\frac{3}{16}$ in. from the edge, as shown in figure 4. Then reduce the bulb to an octagon and round it as shown. To shape the long section between C and E, measure in from both edges on all four sides, $\frac{3}{8}$ in. at C, $\frac{5}{16}$ in. at D, and $\frac{9}{32}$ in. at E, and tick off pencil marks. Then use a wooden batten to connect these marks into continuous lines from D to E (figure 5). The octagon lines C to D are drawn freehand. Before cutting these bevels down to the guidelines, make short, beveled chisel cuts at C to outline the octagon shape and prevent tear out.

How well you round the leg from one end to the other depends primarily on how accurately you cut the bevels. And this, in turn, depends on taking off only a little wood at a time. If you have a really light touch, you can use a drawknife, but

the finer-cutting spokeshave is safer. True up and smooth all surfaces with a 10-in. double cut, flat bastard file, being careful not to nick the shoulders at C and the bulb at E.

Next, work the foot end of the leg (F to G) to size, making it square in section. Then lay out the octagon lines with the same measurement as for E, and cut the bevels as above. Follow the same general procedure to round the leg at G, below the bulb.

The next stage in rounding the leg is to chamfer the eight sides to make 16. You do this strictly by eye with a 10-in. file, again working away from the high point at D. File one or two edges, then work the others to match. Make a cardboard contour template from the original pattern to guide you. Hold it on one edge of the

lathebox, rotate the leg, and pencil mark any imperfections to be filed off.

Shape the top of the leg, B to C, in the same way. Lay out octagon lines $\frac{7}{16}$ in. from the edges. Chamfer the eight edges, as before, to make 16. Continue filing to make the leg cylindrical.

Pick up the dimensions for the two rings from the pattern and lay them out by holding a pencil on the mark while you slowly rotate the leg in the lathebox. Next, saw $\frac{1}{16}$ in. deep on these lines. Put one corner of the 10-in. file in the kerf (figure 6) and rotate the leg to make a V-shaped trough. Do the other ring the same way, then file both rings to shape, as you did with the bulb.

When all the roughing out is completed, spin the leg round smartly several times in the lathebox to watch it in mo-

---

Fig. 5: Octagon shaping
drawing the octagon lines

wooden batten

tick marks

G F E

D C

beveled chisel cuts to outline octagon

C D

octagonal shaping completed from C to E

rings

G F E

D C B

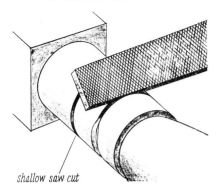

shallow saw cut

tion. Mark any glaring bulges and flat places with a soft pencil, then file away the marks and a bit of wood. Continue the process over the length of the leg from B to E, filing with patience and restraint—as the work is close to the point where no spare wood remains. To assist in this refinement, make a template to check diameters at three or four fixed points along the leg.

When everything looks shipshape, switch from the file to 220-grit sandpaper. Wrap the paper around a thin, flat stick and sand lightly with one hand down and across the leg at a slight angle as you slowly rotate the leg with the other. Now go back over the leg and use the flat and the thin edges of a fine, half-round file to sharpen the tight areas that the coarser tools can't reach—the shoulder at B, the groove between the rings, the junction at C and the sections above and below the bulb. For a more polished surface, shoeshine up and down the leg with a 1-in. strip of 220- or 320-grit sandpaper backed with masking tape. Cut off the 1-in. waste from the top and bottom of the leg in a miter box.

No matter how carefully you work from the square to octagonal to round, there will probably be a swelling here or an out-of-round section there. Yet, if each step has been measured, marked out and cut accurately and slowly, your turning will be remarkably uniform, and will have the stamp of your own personality. □

Adapted from Furniture Making Plain and Simple, *by Aldren A. Watson and Theodora A. Poulos. ©1984 by Aldren A. Watson and Theodora A. Poulos. Reprinted with permission of the publisher, W. W. Norton & Co., New York. Watson is an illustrator and long-time woodworker living in North Hartland, Vt. Theodora Poulos, is a former editor for a New York publishing firm.*

Pine dressing table

Your handturned legs will transform this simple pine dressing table into an elegant piece of furniture. Referring to the plan, cut all the parts to size. Drill holes for the drawbore pins, then chop the leg mortises. Cut and fit the rail tenons and drill their drawbores.

Before assembling the legs and rails, cut the halved joints on the underside of the drawer rail, one at each end, as shown on the facing page. The front ends of the drawer runners will fit into these joints. As a decorative touch, plane a ¾-in.-wide chamfer along the outside corners of the front legs.

Assembly begins with the sides. Lay a back leg on a piece of carpet or a towel to protect the turning. Insert a side rail into the leg mortise, then push firmly in place to close the joint. Lay a front leg on top of the upended rail, start the mortise-and-tenon joint together and tap the leg down with your fist. After clamping the joints, start the drawbore pins into one leg and drive them home with a hammer, tapping one, then the other to draw the joint up evenly. Pin the other leg, then assemble the second side. Join the back rail and drawer rail to the side units in the same way.

Turn the table upside down and attach the drawer runners with countersunk screws. Stand the table upright and clamp the drawer guides on top of the runners, aligning their inside edges flush with the inside faces of the front legs. Fasten them with countersunk screws.

The drawer is joined with dovetails at the front and dowel pins at the back. Cut ¼-in. rabbets in the sides and front to house the plywood bottom. Slide the plywood into the rabbets and nail it to the edge of the drawer back. After attaching the drawer pulls, put the drawer in place with its front flush with the front edge of the drawer rail. Without moving the drawer, mark the back of the drawer on the runners and attach the stops there.

Next, edge-glue two boards to make the top and cut the front corners at a 45° angle as shown. Then lay the top face down on the bench. Set the table frame bottom-side up on it and adjust until there's an even overhang at the front and both ends, and a ½-in. gap at the back for the backboard. Position the cleats by drawing a line on the tabletop around the inside of the frame. Remove the frame and screw the cleats inside the marks. Set the frame down over the cleats and screw each cleat to the side rails.

Cut the scrolls on the backboard with a coping or scroll saw, smoothing the curves with a file, spokeshave, and sandpaper. Screw the backboard to the rear edge of the tabletop and attach two cleats to the back for support. Now you're ready to finish the table, as you like. —A.A.W.

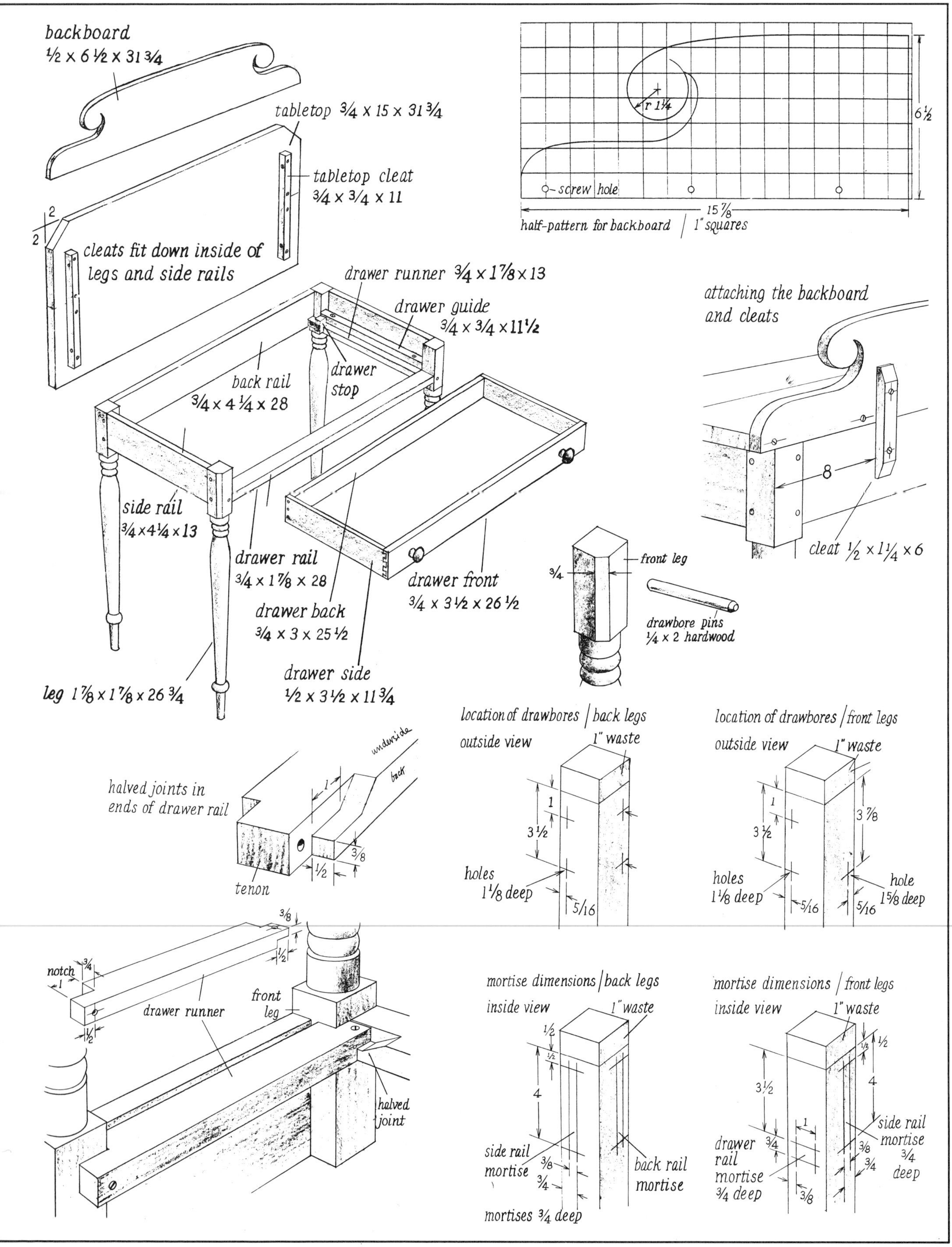
backboard
1/2 x 6 1/2 x 31 3/4
tabletop 3/4 x 15 x 31 3/4
tabletop cleat
3/4 x 3/4 x 11
2
2
cleats fit down inside of legs and side rails
drawer runner 3/4 x 1 7/8 x 13
drawer guide
3/4 x 3/4 x 11 1/2
drawer stop
back rail
3/4 x 4 1/4 x 28
side rail
3/4 x 4 1/4 x 13
drawer rail
3/4 x 1 7/8 x 28
drawer front
3/4 x 3 1/2 x 26 1/2
drawer back
3/4 x 3 x 25 1/2
drawer side
1/2 x 3 1/2 x 11 3/4
leg 1 7/8 x 1 7/8 x 26 3/4
r 1 1/4
6 1/2
screw hole
15 7/8
half-pattern for backboard / 1" squares
attaching the backboard and cleats
8
cleat 1/2 x 1 1/4 x 6
3/4
front leg
drawbore pins
1/4 x 2 hardwood
halved joints in ends of drawer rail
underside
back
1
3/8
1/2
tenon
location of drawbores / back legs
outside view
1" waste
1
3 1/2
holes
1 1/8 deep
5/16
location of drawbores / front legs
outside view
1" waste
1
3 1/2
3 7/8
holes
1 1/8 deep
5/16
hole
1 5/8 deep
5/16
3/8
1/2
notch
3/4
1
drawer runner
front leg
1/2
halved joint
mortise dimensions / back legs
inside view
1" waste
1/2
1/2
4
side rail mortise
3/8
3/4
back rail mortise
mortises 3/4 deep
mortise dimensions / front legs
inside view
1" waste
1/2
1/2
3 1/2
4
1
drawer rail mortise
3/4 deep
3/4
3/8
side rail mortise
3/4 deep
3/8
3/4

Tapered Legs on a Jointer

by Eric Schramm

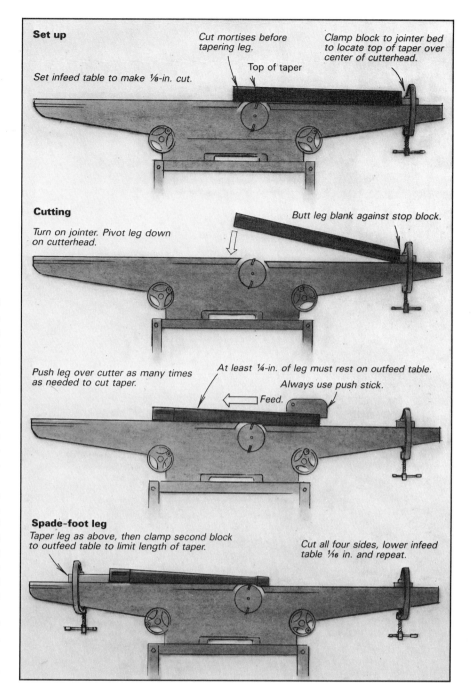

Set up

Cut mortises before tapering leg.

Top of taper

Clamp block to jointer bed to locate top of taper over center of cutterhead.

Set infeed table to make ⅛-in. cut.

Cutting

Butt leg blank against stop block.

Turn on jointer. Pivot leg down on cutterhead.

Push leg over cutter as many times as needed to cut taper.

At least ¼-in. of leg must rest on outfeed table.

Always use push stick.

Feed.

Spade-foot leg

Taper leg as above, then clamp second block to outfeed table to limit length of taper.

Cut all four sides, lower infeed table ¹⁄₁₆ in. and repeat.

If the turned legs on the pine table shown on p. 79 don't suit your fancy, you might want to build the piece with elegant tapered legs. I cut them with several passes on my jointer, which I fit with stop blocks to set the length of the taper and regulate the slope of cut. This method is fast, accurate and produces smooth surfaces. You could also taper the legs with a bandsaw or tablesaw, then finish with a smoothing plane, which is what I do with very short tapers rather than trying to pull small pieces over the cutterhead.

For a table like this I begin with 1¾-in. stock and taper it on all four sides to ⅞ in. Before you begin cutting, draw the taper on all four faces of the leg and carry the guidelines onto the bottom end of the leg so they remain visible after you start cutting. It's also easier to cut the leg mortises above the taper in the square stock before you begin shaping.

If you're tapering stock that's shorter than the length of the infeed table, set up the jointer as shown *before* starting the machine. Lower the infeed table to make a ⅛-in. cut. Place the stock on top of the infeed table and against the fence with its top section resting on the edge of the outfeed table. Butt a stop block against the end of the leg and clamp the block to the infeed table.

Now, remove the leg and start the jointer. Place the bottom end of the leg against the stop block, carefully open the blade guard wide enough for the leg to slide by and lower the leg until the top end rests on the outfeed table. Setting the top of the leg on the outfeed table like this will hold the end high, so that the cut will be tapered toward the other end of the stock as you push the leg through the jointer with the push stick. *Be very careful.* Don't use

the jointer without a push stick. Mine is a 6-in. by 4-in. block of wood notched on one long edge to fit over the leg. Continue cutting each side in turn, until the end is tapered to the guidelines you've laid out. Then plane or sand to smooth the transition from the square stock to the taper.

If the leg is to be tapered from end to end, you must leave extra length at the top of the leg and adjust the stop block to prevent the leg from missing the edge of the outfeed table. At least ¼ in. of the leg must be on the outfeed table to prevent the leg from dropping onto the cutterhead and kicking back. If the stock is longer than

the infeed table, you can use the same procedure outlined above, if you attach a movable extension that can be moved along with the infeed table.

If you want to make a spade-foot leg or another form requiring a stopped taper, taper leg as above, then attach a second stop block to the outfeed table. Repeat the procedure using the second block to stop the cut. After tapering each side, lower the infeed table about ¹⁄₁₆ in. and cut each side again. Repeat until the foot is formed. □

Eric Schramm designs and builds custom furniture in Los Gatos, Calif.

A Child's Pole Lathe

Foot-powered way to teach woodturning

by John and Jon Leeke

The flying chips and smooth round shapes of lathe work in my shop sparked my then-9-year-old son Jon's interest in woodworking. He wanted to get started on the lathe right away. I wanted to say yes, but I thought he was too inexperienced to handle the hazards of power equipment. I know I had to act fast, before his interest waned, so I built this simple foot-powered pole lathe and had Jon set up and turning in half a day.

Like all lathes, the pole lathe holds the turning blank between two metal points called centers. The stock is turned by a rope that passes from a foot treadle below, up and around the blank, and on up to the end of a springy pole. The pole keeps tension on the rope so it grips the wood. Pressing down on the treadle with your foot rotates the wood, which goes around several times and then stops when the treadle hits the ground. Lift your foot, and the pole pulls the rope back up, the blank goes backwards, and you're set for another down stroke. Since the turning action is intermittent, it takes some coordination to cut only on the down stroke.

To save time and space in the shop, I built this lathe as an attachment to Jon's workbench. The body of the lathe is gripped by the left vise. The treadle pivots on a bolt in the back leg. To ten-

Photos: John Leeke

A pole lathe is a good way to learn turning basics without the speed or danger of a power lathe. Leeke's simple lathe clamps to his son's workbench. To cut, you push down on the treadle to spin the stock, the springy pole spins it back again and lifts up the treadle, ready for another cut. A rope wrapped around the stock makes it spin. On the cutting stroke, the stock rotates into the gouge; when the pole pulls the treadle up, the stock rotates in the other direction.

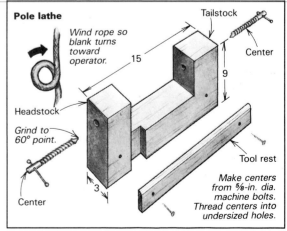

Pole lathe

Wind rope so blank turns toward operator.

Tailstock

Center

15

9

Headstock

Grind to 60° point.

3

Center

Tool rest

Make centers from ⅝-in. dia. machine bolts. Thread centers into undersized holes.

From *Fine Woodworking* magazine (January 1986) 56:76-77

sion the rope, we usually clamp a pole to the back of the bench, but we've used a coil spring hooked to the rafters of the shop as an alternative. You could build the lathe as a free-standing unit or even build an adult-size pole lathe. Old pole lathes sometimes had movable tailstocks. A slotted tenon on the bottom of the tailstock extended down between the two wooden ways that formed the lathe bed and locked in place with a wedge through the slot.

On our version there's no sliding tailstock to bring up against the work, but threaded centers let you chuck and remove wood easily and allow some adjustment for length. The centers are made from ⅝-in. machine bolts. I ground the ends to a 60° point on a bench grinder. The points don't have to be perfectly conical, but they should be close. The surface of the cone should be polished with emery cloth to reduce friction between the center and the turning wood.

I bandsawed the body of the lathe from a piece of cherry. Then, I cut a wide notch along the side of the base to make a space for the rope. I drilled holes in the headstock and tailstock for the centers, just slightly smaller in diameter than the ⅝-in. threads. When I wrenched the centers into the holes they formed their own threads in the wood. The maple tool rest screws to the headstock and tailstock, and ties the two uprights firmly together.

Using the Lathe—To chuck the blank, mark the middle of each end with a pencil. Then, twist the rope around the wood once,

or twice with wood less than 1 in. dia. Press the center mark on one end of the wood onto the sharp point of a lathe center and hold it there. Go to the other end. Line up the center mark with the other center and tighten both centers until you can't turn them any more. Then, loosen them until the wood swivels freely but not loosely. If the blank catches a little on the tool rest, trim it with a chisel.

Push down on the treadle, the top of the blank should turn toward you. If not, twist the rope around the stock in the other direction. Pump some more and watch the wood spin. At first it might seem awkward, but in a few days you will get used to it. After roughing the square blank into a cylinder, remove it and reverse ends to cut down the rough stock where the rope was.

The slow speed of this lathe made it easy for Jon to see and feel just what was happening at the cutting edge of his chisel, and thereby make corrections in the angle of the chisel before the work was spoiled. He easily learned to make nice paring cuts with the skew chisel that left an even, smooth surface on his turnings.

My son worked on the pole lathe for two years. The lathe gave him an excellent background in the skills of woodturning. He now works on the power lathe and can concentrate on safety and more complex projects. □

John Leeke makes furniture in Sanford, Me. Jon Leeke is a high-school student and writes science fiction.

Tips from the Turning Conference

by Rick Mastelli

Equip a shop with 20 lathes and a slide projector. What better way to keep woodturners happy for a weekend? Add a room with tables to display their work and a nearby Holiday Inn where they can wash off the day's shavings and you have the makings of the

seventh semi-annual woodturning symposium at the George School woodshop, Newtown, Pa., June 22 - 24, 1979. On hand were six instructors, several resource persons and 50 participants.

Production woodturner Ray Huskey, of Gatlinburg, Tenn., offered a bag of tricks including using an ice pick for scribing and delicate parting. It's perfect for undercutting a small bevel on the bottom of salt and pepper shakers, which he turns from drilled blanks pressed onto a tapered-spindle faceplate. He also described how to hold stock between centers by compression, an idea that allows you to turn plates without screw or spindle holes.

Rude Osolnik of Berea, Ky., head of the Southern Highland Handicraft

Guild, brought years of experience at the lathe. He demonstrated, for the production turner, form-cutting tools shaped to make checkers, chess pieces or any other simple shape in quantity. □

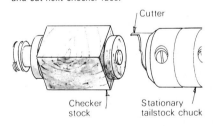

Cut checker face by cranking tailstock in onto end of stock, part off checker and cut next checker face.

Cutter

Checker stock

Stationary tailstock chuck

Spindle-held stock

Drill hole to fit over tapered spindle.

Shaker blank

Tapered spindle

Acorn shaker

Screw faceplate

Ice pick cuts bevel relief for cork plug.

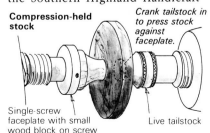

Compression-held stock

Crank tailstock in to press stock against faceplate.

Single-screw faceplate with small wood block on screw

Live tailstock

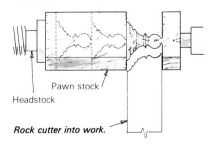

Contour-ground steel cuts simple shapes repeatedly. Then chop pieces off.

Pawn stock

Headstock

Rock cutter into work.

Ringed Rattle
Old turner's trick makes child's toy

by Richard Starr

Photos: Richard Starr

This neat little toy interests adults almost as much as it pleases kids. It's pretty to look at and fun to handle—the loose rings bump along the beaded shaft with a gentle clatter. Grownups wonder how the rings got onto the one-piece handle and shaft. Some even try to undo the puzzle, but the rings won't come off because they were turned in place. It's an old trick: A beautiful 6th-century B.C. wooden chalice unearthed in a Celtic burial site in Germany had free rings turned around its base.

The rattle in the photographs is about 6 in. long; I made it from stock about 8 in. long and 2 in. in diameter. Make yours any size with any number of rings, but avoid toxic or irritating woods such as African blackwood, wenge or cocobolo, and finish it with mineral oil; this toy is likely to be put in baby's mouth.

EDITOR'S NOTE: Another good old trick is to break one ring, interlock it with another, and glue the break. They'll never figure it out.

2. Undercut the ring from both sides using the toe of a sharp ¼-in. skew. A paring cut leaves a smooth surface, but be careful not to free the ring yet.

3. Sand the accessible surfaces of the ring; I use 220 and 400-grit wet/dry paper, kept wet with mineral oil.

1. To begin, cut two grooves near the end of the stock with a parting tool, leaving the wood between them a bit wider than the first ring will be. Turn down the end of the stock to about 1 in. in diameter, then widen the space to the left of the ring with a gouge. I like to graduate the ring diameters so the middle ring looks as if it would fall off the rattle, were it not retained by the smaller rings. To do this, reduce the diameter of the first ring, then round its crest with a gouge or beading tool.

4. Free the ring by undercutting from both sides with the toe of the ¼-in. skew, keeping the edge horizontal and the handle down. Try to cut the inside diameter of the ring as large as possible.

From *Fine Woodworking* magazine (November 1979) 19:58-59

5. Use the same procedure to cut and free the rest of the rings; be sure to sand the surfaces before freeing each ring.

6. Shape the ball on the end of the rattle, leaving it just a little larger than the inside diameter of the first ring.

7. Use a ½-in. skew to trim the shaft to a smooth cylinder, but leave the diameter of the shaft as large as possible at this stage. Hold the rings away from the tool with your finger.

8. Wrap a strip of sandpaper around the shaft clockwise (so it doesn't unwind in use) and hold it in place with a rubber band. If the inner surfaces of the ring are ragged, start with 100-grit paper.

9. With the lathe running, hold each ring against the sandpaper. Move the ring to sand every section of the inside surface evenly, and tilt it to round the edges. I work up to 400-grit wet/dry paper wetted with mineral oil.

10. This is a good time to rough out the shape of the handle. Then trim the shaft to its finished diameter and lay out the beads with deep marks cut with the point of the ¼-in. skew.

11. Use the toe of the skew or a beading tool to cut the beads. Shape the handle, then sand everything with wet/dry paper and mineral oil. Saw the waste off the ends, whittle them smooth, sand and oil. Warning: This rattle may be habit-forming. Don't leave it around unsupervised adults.   □

The Mysterious Celt

Behold the mysterious celt,
With a property that amuses.
One way it will spin,
The other way it refuses.

by Allan J. Boardman

Many thousands of years ago, some nameless neolithic craftsman fashioned a chopping implement from stone. Based on the Latin word for chisel, *celtis,* such tools are called celts (soft "c"). But for some reason, the nearly symmetrical shape of this particular celt incorporated a subtle distortion that gave it a peculiar dynamical property. When spun on a smooth surface, it turned freely in one direction; spun the other way it wobbled, rattled and reversed its direction. Not all celts exhibit this odd property.

The odd motion of some celts inspires many who see it to suggest that the explanation is magnetism, aerodynamics, the Coriolis effect or some form of trickery. A few look at it and say, "So what." In reality, the behavior is a function of the celt's shape, as is its free-spinning direction—clockwise or counterclockwise. I have made more than a hundred celts from a variety of materials, but mostly from wood, and each one has individual idiosyncrasies. Some are less than 2 in. in length, others are over 1 ft. long; some reverse direction several times before stopping.

Once a few important points are understood, it isn't difficult to make one of these curiosities. The exact shape can be mathematically derived, but trial-and-error is easier and, for woodworkers at least, more enjoyable. The general shape, size and proportions can vary considerably, but where the celt contacts the table, the configuration is critical and its surface must be very smooth.

Select a piece of dense hardwood about 5 in. long, 1 in. wide and ¾ in. thick. I prefer rosewood, ebony, lignum vitae or desert ironwood. Finish the top surface flat and smooth. Lay out the outline shown in figure 1 and saw to shape. With a rasp, sanding disc or knife, round the bottom surface as symmetrically as possible. As the shape develops, check for symmetry and balance by placing the piece on a tabletop to detect tilt. Carefully correct any lopsidedness. When the blank is balanced, sandpaper to a very fine finish—the objective at this stage is graceful curves, smoothness, balance and symmetry, so that when the piece is sitting still, its flat top is parallel to the table.

At this point you may have already produced a celt, having unwittingly created one of the infinite number of shapes that will work. Spin it both ways—it should exhibit very little friction and its behavior should be different in each direction. If it spins freely both clockwise and counterclockwise, you were too successful in your attempt at symmetry—but fear not.

The next step is to deliberately upset the symmetry in a par-

Fig. 1: The celt blank

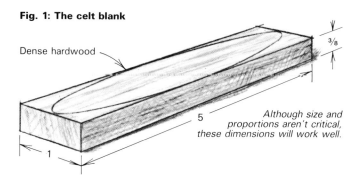

Dense hardwood

⅜

5

1

Although size and proportions aren't critical, these dimensions will work well.

Fig. 2: Proper balance

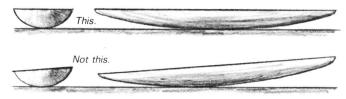

This.

Not this.

Fig. 3: Shaping the bottom

Imaginary line along "keel."

Asymmetry has been greatly exaggerated for clarity.

Fig. 4: Turning celts on the lathe

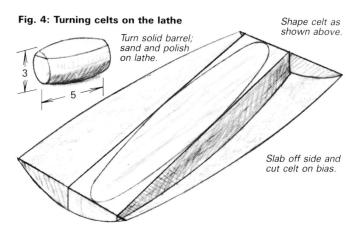

Shape celt as shown above.

Turn solid barrel; sand and polish on lathe.

3

5

Slab off side and cut celt on bias.

From *Fine Woodworking* magazine (July 1985) 53:68-69

Tip tops

by Girvan Milligan

Like most woodworkers, I have a large accumulation of wood scraps. At times I think of them as kindling, but then I remember all the useful and playful things I've made from scrap and how scarce and expensive solid wood is becoming. Tops are fun to make and to play with, and save some of the scraps from the firewood pile.

The idea of making tops came when my granddaughter showed up with a rather poorly-made top that cried out for improvement. I started by gluing up a stack of ¾-in. stock to make a turning block like the one shown in the drawing. (This makes a pretty hefty top; make smaller blocks for smaller tops.) I learned from my granddaughter's top that balance is *all* in a top, so I was careful to make the stack from wood that was as uniform as possible. After trimming waste on the bandsaw, I centered the stem portion on a ½-in. dia. live tailstock center and simply turned the stem down to the center's diameter.

Top shape is largely a matter of choice, but whatever the shape, turn a 1-in. shoulder at the top of the body to provide a bearing surface for the handle. Sand the top between centers, then turn the bottom to a fairly blunt point before parting off with a skew. For a more durable point, you can insert a 1 in. length of ¼-in. bronze brazing rod in the bottom after rounding the rod end in the drill press.

The handle is a three-piece lamination made of the same ¾-in. stock as the top. Drill the ⁹⁄₁₆-in. hole for the stem before cutting away the waste and shaping the handle. Remember, children's hands are small.

Bore a ⅛-in. hole for the string in the

Tops are splendid projects for recycling scrap. This one is made of birch plywood.

middle of the stem and cut the stem flush with the top arm of the handle. To finish the top, I submerge it in Watco oil until the bubbles stop appearing. Attach the string—nylon masons' line works well—to a toggle to give a good grip.

To spin the top, put the stem in the handle, thread the string an inch or so through the hole, hold the top horizontally and turn it to wind the string onto the stem. On a smooth surface, hold the top by the handle and *pull*. Lift off the handle and watch the top go! □

Girvan Milligan is a woodworker in Carmel, N.Y. Photo by the author.

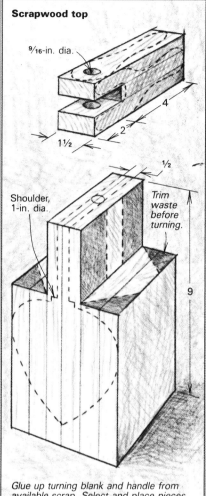

Scrapwood top

⁹⁄₁₆-in. dia.

4

2

1½

½

Shoulder, 1-in. dia.

Trim waste before turning.

9

Glue up turning blank and handle from available scrap. Select and place pieces so top will be well balanced.

---

ticular way to achieve the behavior we're looking for. To do this, file, scrape or sandpaper diagonally opposite quadrants of the celt's bottom, as though you were making it slightly propeller-like. Figure 3, facing page, illustrates this—greatly exaggerated for clarity. Be careful not to remove too much wood, and be sure to maintain diagonal symmetry. This propeller-like distortion should be barely perceptible in the finished celt. Again, test on a tabletop. You'll have to smooth the bottom to a high degree to test both for balance and to see if you have arrived at the desired shape. You may not get it the first time, but keep trying. Experimentation will reveal how subtle variations will affect the spinning motion, the liveliness and the reversing properties. When you're satisfied with the celt's performance, a slight chamfer or rounding of the edge and a bit of oil or wax will finish it.

My friend, Jerry Glaser, developed a method for making a celt on the lathe, which is illustrated in figure 4. The bottom surface is sort of automatically produced, and the same turned barrel can make two or three additional celts.

In general, the smaller the celt, the faster it will rattle and reverse. The larger models have a sluggish, lumbering behavior.

Why does the celt do what it does? Simply put, a dynamic imbalance excites an instability that transfers its energy to a wobbling motion which, in turn, induces a counter rotation. Or maybe it's magnetism. As far back as the 1890s, mathematical and descriptive treatises have been written about the celt.

The celt has been called by other names—"wobblestone" and "rattleback," for example. One particularly interesting name, "tates," is said to originate from the little-known historical fact that prehistoric Celtic (hard "c") people used this object as a navigational compass. When the tates was spun, it would ultimately come to rest pointing in a completely arbitrary direction—a different direction each time. Obviously, as a compass, the tates was a dud. But the valiant, if unsuccessful, effort of this early people to harness natural phenomena did give rise to an important adage in common usage to this day: He who has a tates is lost. □

Allan J. Boardman, of Woodland Hills, Calif., is an amateur woodworker and a corporate officer in an aerospace firm. For a scientific explanation of the celt, see "The Mysterious 'Rattleback'" by Jearl Walker, Scientific American, October 1979.

Index

FINE WOODWORKING
Editorial Staff, 1975-1986

Paul Bertorelli
Mary Blaylock
Dick Burrows
Jim Cummins
Katie de Koster
Ruth Dobsevage
Tage Frid
Roger Holmes
Cindy Howard
John Kelsey
Linda Kirk
Nancy-Lou Knapp
John Lively
Rick Mastelli
Nina Perry
Jim Richey
Paul Roman
David Sloan
Nancy Stabile
Laura Tringali
Linda D. Whipkey

FINE WOODWORKING
Art Staff, 1975-1986

Roger Barnes
Kathleen Creston
Deborah Fillion
Lee Hov
Betsy Levine
Lisa Long
E. Marino III
Karen Pease
Roland Wolf

FINE WOODWORKING
Production Staff, 1975-1986

Claudia Applegate
Barbara Bahr
Jennifer Bennett
Pat Byers
Mark Coleman
Deborah Cooper
Kathleen Davis
David DeFeo
Michelle Fryman
Mary Galpin
Dinah George
Barbara Hannah
Annette Hilty
Margot Knorr
Jenny Long
Johnette Luxeder
Gary Mancini
Laura Martin
Mary Eileen McCarthy
JoAnn Muir
Cynthia Lee Nyitray
Kathryn Olsen
Mary Ann Snieckus
Barbara Snyder